A.A. Castor

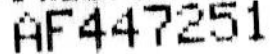

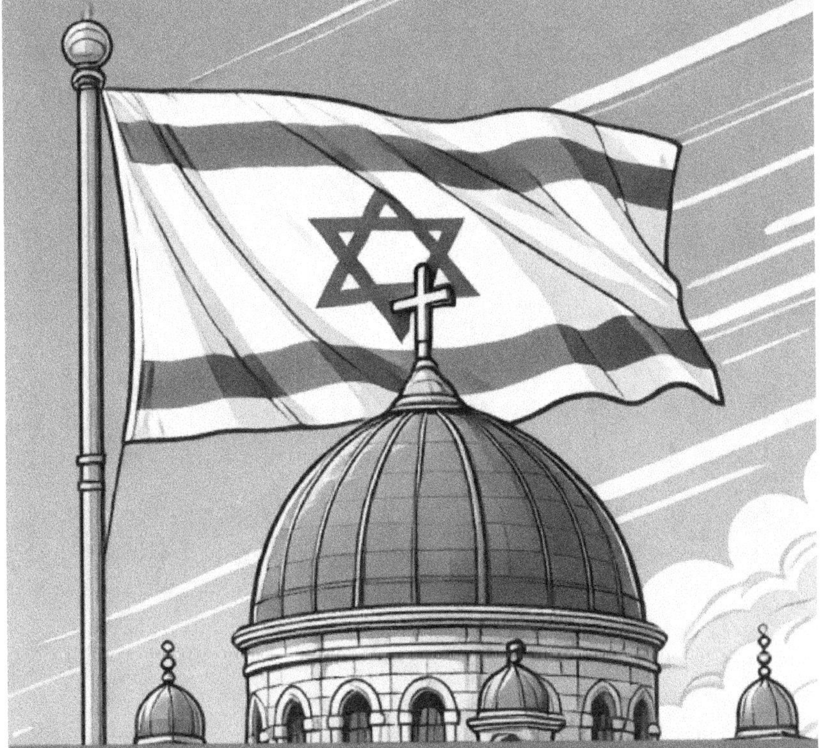

Crosses in the Crossfire

The Christian Battle for Existence in Occupied Palestine

Table of Contents

Crosses in the Crossfire: The Christian Battle for Existence in Occupied Palestine

A.A. Castor

Dedication

To my beloved family,

Your unconditional love, unwavering support, and endless encouragement have been my greatest blessings. From the earliest days of dreaming to the challenging moments of writing, you have stood by me with patience and belief. This book is as much yours as it is mine, a reflection of the values you've instilled and the faith you've shown in me. Thank you for being my rock and my inspiration.

To my dear friends,

Your friendship has illuminated my path with laughter, shared moments, and invaluable support. You've cheered me on through every triumph and lifted me up through every challenge. Your belief in my endeavors has been a source of strength and motivation. This book is a testament to the power of friendship, and I am grateful for each of you who has walked this journey by my side.

To God,

Your grace and guidance have been my constant companions. In moments of doubt, you've shown me the way; in moments of joy, you've multiplied my gratitude. This book is a testament to your faithfulness and the blessings you've bestowed upon me. May it serve as a reflection of your love and the lessons you continue to teach me.

With heartfelt gratitude and love,

A.A. Castor

Copyright © 2024 by A.A. Castor

All rights reserved. No part of this book may be reproduced, stored in a retrieval system, or transmitted in any form or by any means—electronic, mechanical, photocopy, recording, scanning, or otherwise—except as permitted under Section 107 or 108 of the 1976 United States Copyright Act, without the prior written permission of the publisher, except for brief quotations embodied in critical reviews and certain other noncommercial uses permitted by copyright law.

For permission requests, contact A.A. Castor at:

Address: Urban Deca Home Metro Manila, 1230

Email: dev.castortony@gmail.com

Website: www.tonyc.info[1]

This book is a work of non-fiction. Names, characters, places, and incidents are either the product of the author's research or are used factually. Any resemblance to actual persons, living or dead, events, or locales is entirely coincidental.

Printed in Philippines

Philippine Copyright Law:

The Intellectual Property Code of the Philippines (Republic Act No. 8293) provides protection to literary and artistic works from the moment of their creation. It includes provisions for the rights of authors and copyright owners, including the exclusive right to reproduce, distribute, perform, and display their works. Unauthorized use or reproduction of copyrighted materials is subject to legal penalties under this law.

---

1. http://www.tonyc.info

Why I Am Writing This Book

The story of Palestinian Christians is one that has long been overshadowed by the broader narratives of the Israeli-Palestinian conflict. As a global Christian, I feel a deep responsibility to bring attention to the struggles of my brothers and sisters in the Holy Land, many of whom are facing marginalization, displacement, and the loss of their religious heritage. This book is my way of shedding light on their plight, highlighting the challenges they endure, and calling for a renewed commitment to their survival and dignity.

I am writing this book because I believe that the global Christian community has a moral and spiritual duty to stand in solidarity with Palestinian Christians. For too long, the focus has been on political and religious divisions that overlook the human cost borne by Christians living in the land where our faith was born. Palestinian Christians are not only guardians of holy sites but also living testimonies to the enduring presence of Christianity in the region. Their perseverance in the face of occupation and adversity is an inspiration, but it is also a reminder that their continued existence is under threat. I am compelled to ensure that their voices are heard and their struggles recognized by Christians around the world.

This book also serves as a call to action. I want to encourage Christians outside the Middle East to reconsider their often unquestioning support for policies that harm Palestinian Christians and to reexamine the impact of such positions on their fellow believers. Many in the global Christian community are unaware of the realities on the ground, shaped by theological and political narratives that have overlooked the suffering of Palestinian Christians. Through this book, I aim to provide a clearer picture of their daily hardships, the legal and social structures that oppress them, and the ways in which global Christians can actively participate in supporting their cause.

Ultimately, I am writing this book because I believe that justice and faith are inseparable. As Christians, we are called to stand with those who are oppressed and to advocate for peace and justice in all its forms. Palestinian Christians are calling out for support, and it is our duty to answer that call. By raising awareness, promoting advocacy, and offering meaningful support, we can ensure that Palestinian Christians continue to live, worship, and thrive in the land where Christianity began.

This book is not just a chronicle of suffering; it is also a testament to the resilience, faith, and hope of a community determined to preserve its place in the Holy Land. It is my hope that through these pages, readers will be inspired to take action, to stand in solidarity, and to work towards a future where Palestinian Christians can live with dignity, freedom, and justice.

Warning and Disclaimer

The author and publisher of this book have made every effort to ensure that the information contained within is accurate and up to date. However, the complexities of the Israeli-Palestinian conflict, as well as political, social, and religious sensitivities, mean that the information presented is subject to change and interpretation. The content of this book is intended for informational purposes only and does not constitute legal, political, or professional advice. Readers are encouraged to verify details and consult appropriate experts before making decisions based on the material provided.

The author and publisher are not liable for any errors, omissions, or inaccuracies in the content of this book, nor for any consequences that may arise from its use. Any actions taken based on the information provided in this book are at the reader's own discretion and risk. The views expressed are those of the author and do not necessarily reflect the views of any organizations, individuals, or entities mentioned within the book.

This book is meant to encourage reflection, education, and constructive discussion on a sensitive subject. It is not intended to incite division or hostility but to promote understanding and advocacy for justice.

About the Author

A.A. Castor is a dedicated writer and researcher with a deep passion for exploring the intersection of history, religion, and social justice. His work spans a range of topics, including religious conflicts, leadership, and the preservation of cultural heritage. With a particular interest in the struggles of minority religious communities, Castor's writing often delves into the experiences of those who find themselves on the margins, offering insights into their challenges and resilience.

A.A. Castor has devoted considerable time to studying the historical and modern-day realities of Palestinian Christians, driven by a personal commitment to highlighting their ongoing struggles in the Holy Land. His work draws on extensive research and engagement with local and international voices, blending historical study with a call to action for global Christian solidarity. Through his writing, he aims to raise awareness of the often-overlooked experiences of Palestinian Christians, while advocating for justice, peace, and the preservation of religious and cultural diversity in the region.

In addition to his work on religious and political issues, Castor is also an accomplished author of books on leadership, strategy, and social dynamics, always looking to connect lessons from the past with present-day challenges. His research is characterized by a deep respect for the complexity of historical and contemporary conflicts, as well as a commitment to offering practical insights for readers interested in promoting positive change in the world.

Castor regularly contributes to various platforms and is also a podcast host, where he discusses topics related to leadership, history, and social philosophy. His goal is to inspire readers and listeners to think critically about the world around them and to take action in support of justice, equality, and human dignity.

Faith in a Broken Land: The Forgotten Christian Struggle

In the heart of the world's most sacred region, where ancient histories and religious legacies intertwine, the Christian presence in Palestine and Israel has endured for centuries. The Holy Land, revered by billions of Christians worldwide, holds not only the spiritual heritage of their faith but the living communities who have safeguarded this land's religious significance since the birth of Christianity. These communities, who have lived and worshipped in places like Bethlehem, Jerusalem, and Nazareth for generations, find themselves fighting for survival in a land fractured by conflict and division.

Today, their story is one of marginalization and struggle. The Christian population in Palestine has dwindled drastically, not only due to the ongoing conflict but also because of the systemic policies implemented by Israel. Under the weight of military occupation, land confiscations, and expanding Jewish settlements, Palestinian Christians are being steadily pushed out of the land that they and their ancestors have called home for millennia. The reality of their suffering is often overlooked, overshadowed by the broader Israeli-Palestinian conflict that the world views largely through the lens of Jewish-Muslim tensions.

Israeli laws and military actions have severely restricted the freedom of Palestinian Christians. From the confiscation of church lands to the building of the Separation Wall, which isolates Christian communities and cuts off access to their holy sites, the existence of Palestinian Christians is one of constant oppression. Churches that once thrived as centers of community and faith now struggle to maintain their congregations, as more and more Christians emigrate in search of better lives. The everyday challenges of restricted movement, economic strangulation, and the fear of harassment by Jewish extremists add layers of hardship to a community already fighting for survival.

And yet, perhaps most painful of all is the ignorance of Christians outside the Middle East who remain unaware or indifferent to the suffering of their fellow believers. Many Western Christians, particularly in Europe and the United States, continue to support the state of Israel without understanding the consequences their support has for Palestinian Christians. This blind allegiance, often fueled by political ideologies or theological beliefs, contributes to the ongoing marginalization of the very people they claim to spiritually align with.

As Christian populations in Palestine continue to dwindle, their voices are silenced, and their struggles forgotten. Their faith, once a symbol of resilience and hope in the Holy Land, is now tested daily by the weight of occupation and abandonment. The very land where Christianity was born is slowly becoming a place where Christians can no longer live freely, their heritage and existence under constant threat. This book aims to bring to light the untold story of their survival, to expose the truth behind their suffering, and to challenge the global Christian community to reconsider its stance on the Israeli-Palestinian conflict. The battle for the survival of Christianity in the Holy Land is a battle not just for land or politics, but for the very soul of the Christian faith itself.

The Historical Presence of Christians in the Holy Land

FOR CENTURIES, THE Holy Land has been the spiritual heart of Christianity, where the life, death, and resurrection of Jesus Christ unfolded. From the early days of the faith, Christians have lived in this region, preserving the sacred sites that commemorate their most significant religious events. Bethlehem, where Christ was born; Nazareth, where he was raised; and Jerusalem, where he was crucified and rose again—all are central to the Christian faith, and for generations, Christian communities have played a vital role in maintaining the holiness of these places.

The presence of Christians in Palestine dates back to the time of the apostles, when the faith spread from Jerusalem to surrounding regions. Over centuries, Christian communities grew, building churches, monasteries, and schools that not only celebrated the life of Christ but also became hubs for religious, cultural, and social life. From the Byzantine period to the Crusades, from Ottoman rule to the British Mandate, Christians remained a constant, albeit a minority, in the shifting political and religious landscape of the Holy Land.

The significance of the Holy Land to Christianity is unparalleled. It is the birthplace of the faith, the location of its most sacred events, and the destination of countless pilgrimages. For Christians worldwide, the Holy Land represents a physical connection to the life of Christ and the early church. But for the Christians who live there, it is more than just a spiritual symbol—it is their home. Their churches are not merely historical landmarks; they are places of worship, community, and tradition. Their lives are intertwined with the sacred geography of the region, where every street, hill, and village carries the weight of religious history.

However, the Christian population in Palestine and Israel has faced continuous challenges over the centuries. Despite their deep historical roots, Christians in the Holy Land have often been marginalized by various ruling powers, from the early Islamic caliphates to the Ottoman Empire, and now under Israeli control. Yet, through it all, they have remained, upholding their faith and traditions amidst the difficulties.

Today, their historical presence is under threat like never before. The region's political turmoil, Israeli occupation, and the ever-expanding Jewish settlements have pushed many Christians to emigrate, leaving behind a land that is slowly becoming void of its original Christian inhabitants. These pressures have turned the once-thriving Christian communities into a shrinking minority, struggling to hold on to their religious and cultural identity.

For global Christianity, the Holy Land remains a place of pilgrimage and reverence. But for the local Christians, it is a battleground where their very existence is threatened by external forces that disregard their deep connection to the land. As this book will explore, the survival of these communities is not just about maintaining religious sites; it is about preserving the living faith that has been passed down through generations. The story of Christianity in the Holy Land is not merely a historical one—it is a story of endurance, faith, and the ongoing battle for survival in the face of overwhelming odds.

The Forgotten Struggle: Christian Suffering in the Shadows of Israeli Control

IN THE HEART OF THE Holy Land, where Christianity was born, the Christian communities of Palestine find themselves increasingly marginalized and oppressed. For decades, these communities have faced mounting challenges, not just from the overarching conflict between Israelis and Palestinians, but from a system that places them in a state of constant hardship and erasure. Israeli laws and Jewish dominance over key aspects of life in Palestine have created an environment where Christians are not only forgotten but are systematically oppressed, their rights trampled, and their existence threatened.

Under Israeli rule, Christians endure a range of abuses that make their daily lives a struggle for survival. From the confiscation of their lands to discriminatory laws that limit their freedom of movement, the Israeli government has imposed a series of policies that directly impact Christian communities. The Separation Wall cuts through the landscape, dividing Christian towns and families, while military checkpoints and restrictions make it nearly impossible for them to move freely, work, or worship. The encroachment of Jewish settlements onto historically Christian lands has displaced families, robbed them of their livelihoods, and left their future uncertain.

One of the most significant blows to Palestinian Christians is the systematic seizure of their land. Israeli laws, such as the Absentee Property Law, allow the state to confiscate land that belongs to Palestinians—including Christians—if they are deemed to have been absent from it. This has resulted in large portions of Christian-owned land being taken over by the Israeli state or sold to Jewish settlers, who further encroach on these communities. Churches, monasteries, and Christian institutions have also faced similar threats, with properties either seized or subjected to heavy legal battles that drain their resources and weaken their ability to function.

At the same time, many Christians outside the Middle East remain woefully unaware of the suffering their Palestinian brothers and sisters endure. In Western countries, particularly in the United States and Europe, Christians often blindly support the state of Israel, believing it to be a Biblical imperative or a political necessity. This support, however, comes at a great cost to the Christians of Palestine, who are left isolated and abandoned by the very people who share their faith. Christian Zionism, which advocates unwavering support for Israel based on Biblical prophecy, ignores the reality of the occupation and the suffering of Palestinian Christians, further alienating them in their time of need.

The ignorance of global Christianity toward the plight of Palestinian Christians deepens the sense of betrayal felt by those who live under Israeli occupation. While millions of Christians worldwide visit Israel as pilgrims, eager to walk in the footsteps of Christ, they often do so without realizing the pain and hardship endured by the Christians who live there. The churches they visit, the sacred sites they revere, are maintained by communities struggling to survive under oppression, yet their stories are rarely heard or understood by those who travel from afar.

This forgotten struggle is central to the theme of this book. The suffering of Palestinian Christians under Israeli laws and Jewish dominance, coupled with the indifference of global Christian communities, paints a stark picture of a faith community that is slowly being erased from the land where it began. Through land confiscation, economic marginalization, and legal restrictions, Israel has made it increasingly difficult for Christians to remain in the Holy Land. Their struggle for survival, however, is not just a political issue—it is a fight for the preservation of a heritage and a faith that has existed in this land for over two thousand years.

This book seeks to shine a light on that forgotten struggle, to uncover the injustices faced by Palestinian Christians, and to call on global Christians to open their eyes to the suffering of their fellow believers. The narrative of blind support for Israel must be challenged, and the real, human cost of that support must be acknowledged. Palestinian Christians are not just victims of a geopolitical conflict; they are a community under siege, fighting to maintain their identity, their faith, and their right to exist in the land they have called home for generations.

Chapter 1: A History of Christian Struggle in the Holy Land

Christianity's connection to Palestine is as old as the faith itself. It was in this land that Jesus Christ was born, preached, and was crucified, and it is from this land that his message spread to the far reaches of the world. For nearly two thousand years, Christians have maintained a presence in Palestine, safeguarding the sacred sites and nurturing communities that have carried forward the legacy of the early church. The Christian presence in Palestine is not a foreign one; it is indigenous, deeply rooted in the very soil where the faith began. From the first followers of Christ to the Byzantine period, from the Crusades to the Ottoman era, Christians have lived in this land, contributing to its religious and cultural fabric.

However, the Christian story in Palestine is not just one of faith and heritage—it is also one of struggle. Over the centuries, Christians in the region have experienced various forms of marginalization and persecution. Under Roman rule, early Christians were often targeted for their beliefs. Later, during the Crusades, Christian and Muslim forces clashed in brutal wars over control of the Holy Land. Yet, despite these hardships, Christian communities persisted, adapting to the changing political and social landscape while holding fast to their faith.

In more recent times, however, the establishment of the state of Israel in 1948 marked a turning point for the Christians of Palestine. The creation of Israel, followed by the displacement of hundreds of thousands of Palestinians during the Nakba, also deeply affected Christian populations. Many Christians, like their Muslim neighbors, were forced from their homes and lands, becoming refugees in their own country or in neighboring states. Christian communities, once vibrant and integral to the region's diversity, found themselves increasingly marginalized as Israeli policies took hold.

The Israeli occupation that followed the 1967 Six-Day War only deepened the challenges faced by Palestinian Christians. Under Israeli control, Christian communities were subjected to land confiscations, settlement expansion, and legal discrimination. The encroachment of Jewish settlements into historically Christian areas, such as Bethlehem and Beit Jala, has not only displaced Christian families but has also fragmented their communities. Churches and monasteries, once central to the social and spiritual life of these towns, now find themselves surrounded by settlements, cut off from their congregations by walls and military checkpoints.

Israeli policies, such as the Absentee Property Law, have further eroded Christian land ownership. This law allows the state to confiscate land if the owner is not physically present, which has been used to seize large portions of land owned by Christians who fled during times of conflict. Entire neighborhoods and farmlands have been lost, sold to Jewish settlers or absorbed into the expanding territory of Israel. The loss of land, for many Palestinian Christians, is not just an economic blow—it is a spiritual and cultural one, severing their ties to their ancestral homes and to the very land that holds their religious heritage.

The impact of Israeli control over Palestine has been devastating for Christian populations. With their lands taken, their communities divided by walls and barriers, and their access to holy sites restricted, Palestinian Christians have found it increasingly difficult to maintain their presence in the land of their ancestors. Many have been forced to emigrate, seeking better opportunities and greater freedoms abroad. Those who remain face the daily struggle of living under occupation, caught between the harsh realities of Israeli rule and the pressures of a shrinking community.

Yet, through all of this, Palestinian Christians have remained resilient. Their faith endures, even as their numbers dwindle. They continue to maintain their churches, celebrate their traditions, and uphold the Christian presence in a land where their very existence is under threat. The history of Christian struggle in the Holy Land is one of perseverance in the face of overwhelming odds—a testament to the enduring power of faith in a region marked by conflict and division. This chapter explores that history, tracing the deep roots of Christianity in Palestine and examining how the creation of Israel and its policies have systematically harmed Christian populations, displacing communities and threatening their survival in the land where their faith was born.

Christian Roots in Palestine: A Faith Born in the Holy Land

CHRISTIANITY'S ORIGINS are inseparably linked to the land of Palestine, where its foundational events took place. It was here, in this ancient land, that Jesus Christ was born, lived, and carried out his ministry, and it was from here that his teachings spread across the world. Palestine, known today as the Holy Land, became the spiritual and physical heart of Christianity, the place where the first Christians gathered, where the apostles began their mission, and where the faith took its earliest roots. From the humble beginnings of a small group of believers in Jerusalem, Christianity would eventually spread far and wide, but its deep connection to Palestine would remain constant.

In the early days, the Christian community was closely connected to Judaism, with many of the first followers of Christ being Jews who saw Jesus as the fulfillment of messianic prophecy. Jerusalem, the city where Christ was crucified and resurrected, became the first center of Christian worship. The apostles, including Peter and Paul, preached throughout the region, establishing a foundation of faith that would endure for centuries. As the Christian message spread, communities formed in key cities like Nazareth, Bethlehem, and beyond. The early Christians in Palestine lived side by side with other religious groups, marking the land as a diverse but spiritually rich environment.

As the Roman Empire took control of the region, the early Christian community faced periods of persecution, particularly under emperors who viewed the new faith as a threat to Roman religious traditions. Despite these challenges, Christianity continued to grow, and by the fourth century, with Emperor Constantine's conversion and the subsequent Christianization of the Roman Empire, the faith gained a foothold. Constantine's mother, Helena, embarked on a pilgrimage to the Holy Land, leading to the establishment of many of the most important Christian holy sites, including the Church of the Nativity in Bethlehem and the Church of the Holy Sepulchre in Jerusalem. These sites became pilgrimage destinations for Christians worldwide, cementing Palestine's place as the cradle of their faith.

Throughout the Byzantine period, Christianity flourished in Palestine. Monasteries, churches, and religious communities sprang up across the region, attracting scholars, monks, and pilgrims. Cities like Jerusalem and Bethlehem became vibrant centers of Christian life, with theological schools, monastic orders, and charitable institutions. The Christian population grew, and for several centuries, Christians were the dominant religious group in many areas of Palestine. The region's role as a crossroads of faith and culture only deepened with time, as Christians interacted with Jews, Samaritans, and later, Muslims, shaping a diverse religious landscape.

However, the rise of Islam in the 7th century brought significant changes. As Muslim armies expanded into Palestine, the Christian population faced new challenges. Though the Islamic rulers often allowed Christians to continue practicing their faith, they were relegated to dhimmi status, a protected but subordinate class within the Islamic state. Christian communities were required to pay the jizya tax and were limited in their political and social roles, but their religious practices were largely tolerated. Despite these restrictions, many Christian communities adapted to the new political order, maintaining their religious institutions and continuing to worship in the land of Christ.

Over the centuries, Palestine saw a series of rulers—Umayyads, Abbasids, Crusaders, and Ottomans—all of whom left their mark on the Christian population. During the Crusades, the region became the epicenter of a violent struggle between Christians and Muslims for control of Jerusalem and the holy sites. While the Crusader period was marked by bloodshed and turmoil, it also saw the establishment of numerous churches and Christian institutions. Yet, as the Crusader kingdoms fell, Christians once again became a minority under Muslim rule.

Under the Ottoman Empire, which ruled Palestine for centuries, Christians experienced a relatively stable existence. Though they remained a minority, Christian communities continued to thrive in cities like Jerusalem, Nazareth, and Bethlehem. The Ottomans allowed Christian institutions, such as schools, churches, and hospitals, to operate, and Christian pilgrims from around the world continued to visit the Holy Land. Despite the political subordination, Palestinian Christians remained deeply rooted in their faith and their land, playing a vital role in the religious and cultural life of the region.

By the time of the British Mandate in the early 20th century, the Christian population in Palestine had developed strong communal structures, with schools, hospitals, and churches serving as central pillars of their communities. The arrival of European missionaries brought new educational and social opportunities, while Christian religious orders expanded their presence in key cities. However, the political upheaval that followed the end of the British Mandate, and particularly the creation of the state of Israel in 1948, dramatically altered the landscape for Palestinian Christians. Many were displaced alongside their Muslim counterparts during the Nakba, the mass exodus of Palestinians from their homes.

In the decades that followed, the Christian population in Palestine continued to shrink due to the pressures of Israeli occupation, economic hardship, and emigration. While many of the sacred sites remain, the communities that once thrived around them have been steadily eroded. Today, Palestinian Christians are a small, but resilient minority, maintaining their presence in places like Bethlehem, Jerusalem, and Nazareth. Their roots in the region run deep, connecting them to the very origins of their faith, but their future in the Holy Land remains uncertain.

The history of Christianity in Palestine is not just a story of faith; it is a story of endurance. The Christians of this land have weathered centuries of political upheaval, religious persecution, and social marginalization, yet they have remained steadfast in their belief and their connection to the land where their faith began. As this book explores the ongoing struggles they face, it is important to remember the deep roots they have in Palestine and the vital role they have played in shaping the religious and cultural heritage of the Holy Land.

From Coexistence to Occupation: The Marginalization of Christian Communities in Palestine

FOR CENTURIES, CHRISTIAN communities in Palestine coexisted with their Muslim and Jewish neighbors, contributing to the region's rich cultural and religious tapestry. While there were moments of tension throughout history, Christians remained a respected and integral part of Palestinian society. They built churches, schools, and hospitals, and their holy sites became pilgrimage destinations for believers around the world. Christians in Palestine were an active, thriving part of the social fabric, maintaining their faith and traditions in harmony with the region's complex religious dynamics.

However, the establishment of the state of Israel in 1948 dramatically changed the landscape for Palestinian Christians. What had once been a situation of coexistence quickly turned into one of displacement and marginalization. The creation of Israel, along with the wars that followed, resulted in the forced expulsion of hundreds of thousands of Palestinians—both Muslims and Christians—from their homes. Entire Christian towns and villages were emptied as the new Israeli state expanded its borders. Churches that had stood for centuries suddenly found themselves abandoned, and Christian communities were scattered, many becoming refugees overnight.

The Nakba, or "catastrophe," as Palestinians call the events of 1948, left a lasting scar on the Christian population. Alongside their Muslim neighbors, Christians were forced to flee to neighboring countries or relocate to different parts of Palestine, where they struggled to rebuild their lives. This displacement was not just a physical loss of homes and lands; it was also the beginning of a process of systematic marginalization under Israeli control.

As Israel solidified its presence in the region, Christian communities found themselves increasingly sidelined by policies that favored Jewish settlers and systematically excluded Palestinians, regardless of their religion. Israeli laws like the Absentee Property Law allowed the state to confiscate land belonging to Palestinians who had fled, including Christians who had been displaced during the conflict. This law, designed to secure land for the growing Jewish population, resulted in the widespread seizure of Christian-owned properties. Entire neighborhoods that had been predominantly Christian for centuries were now under Israeli control, their former inhabitants unable to return or reclaim what was taken.

For the Christians who remained in Palestine, life under Israeli rule presented new challenges. The military occupation that began after the

1967 Six-Day War further exacerbated the situation. Christian towns like Bethlehem, Beit Jala, and Beit Sahour, once thriving centers of Christian life, became enclosed by Israeli settlements and military checkpoints. The construction of the Separation Wall in the early 2000s physically divided these towns, cutting them off from Jerusalem and other major cities. For many Christians, daily life became a struggle of navigating roadblocks and restricted movement, with access to work, education, and even worship severely limited.

The expansion of Jewish settlements in the West Bank has been particularly devastating for Christian communities. In places like Bethlehem, Christian families have watched as their land has been taken by settlers, their access to farmland and economic resources stripped away. Churches that were once surrounded by Christian homes and families now sit isolated, surrounded by Israeli settlements or military installations. The encroachment of settlers has not only displaced Christian families but has also created a hostile environment where Christians are often subject to harassment and violence by radical settler groups.

Israeli policies have not only targeted land ownership but have also impacted the ability of Christians to practice their faith freely. The bureaucratic system of permits and checkpoints has made it increasingly difficult for Christians to attend religious services or visit holy sites, particularly in Jerusalem. Churches must constantly navigate the complex web of Israeli laws and military regulations, and Christian leaders often face obstacles when attempting to build or renovate religious buildings. The systematic marginalization extends even to the control of holy sites, where Israeli authorities have frequently undermined Christian custodianship, particularly in places like the Church of the Holy Sepulchre in Jerusalem.

As a result of these pressures, many Palestinian Christians have chosen to emigrate. The Christian population in Palestine has declined significantly since the establishment of Israel, and today, they make up a small fraction of what was once a vibrant community. Those who remain are often economically disadvantaged, politically marginalized, and socially isolated. They live in the shadow of a state that increasingly views them as outsiders in the land where their faith was born.

The shift from coexistence to occupation has transformed the lives of Palestinian Christians. Where once they lived alongside their neighbors in relative peace, they now find themselves caught in a system that views them as second-class citizens. The marginalization of Christian communities in Palestine is not just a story of land loss or political disenfranchisement; it is a story of cultural and religious erasure. As Israeli control over the region tightens, the future of Palestinian Christians grows ever more uncertain. Their history of resilience is undeniable, but the pressures they face today threaten the very existence of Christianity in the Holy Land.

This chapter explores the trajectory of that marginalization, from the displacement of 1948 to the ongoing occupation and the expansion of Jewish settlements. It examines how Israeli policies have systematically undermined the presence of Christian communities and questions what the future holds for a faith that is increasingly being driven from the land of its birth.

The Impact of Israeli Control: Displacement and the Seizure of Christian Lands

THE CREATION OF THE state of Israel in 1948 marked a turning point for the Christian populations of Palestine. While the establishment of Israel is often viewed through the lens of Jewish-Muslim conflict, Palestinian Christians were equally affected by the ensuing displacement, loss of land, and military occupation that followed. For generations, Christians had lived on their ancestral lands, maintaining deep connections to the places where their faith was born. However, with the formation of Israel and the subsequent wars and military actions, these communities found themselves uprooted, their lands confiscated, and their future uncertain.

The events of 1948, known to Palestinians as the Nakba, or "catastrophe," saw the forced displacement of hundreds of thousands of Palestinians, including Christians. Entire Christian towns and villages were depopulated as Israeli forces advanced, driving out their inhabitants. Many Christians fled to neighboring countries like Jordan and Lebanon, while others became internally displaced within what remained of Palestine. The chaos and destruction of that time not only tore families from their homes but also shattered the centuries-old presence of Christian communities in key areas like Jaffa, Haifa, and the Galilee.

The impact of Israeli control on Christian populations did not end with the initial displacement. In the decades that followed, Israeli military actions, settlement expansion, and legal measures continued to undermine the stability and survival of Palestinian Christians. One of the most significant tools used to seize Christian lands was the Absentee Property Law, enacted by the Israeli government in the early years of the state's existence. This law allowed Israel to take ownership of properties belonging to Palestinians who had fled or were not physically present, categorizing them as "absentees" and transferring their land to the state. Christian families who had lived on their lands for generations suddenly found themselves unable to return, their homes and farms taken over by Jewish settlers or absorbed into state-controlled areas.

The construction of Israeli settlements in the West Bank, particularly around Christian towns like Bethlehem, Beit Jala, and Beit Sahour, further exacerbated the problem. Settlements rapidly expanded into areas historically owned by Christian families, often with the support and protection of the Israeli military. Christian farmers who once relied on their land for agricultural livelihoods lost access to their fields, either through outright confiscation or by being cut off by security barriers and roads built to serve the settlements. The Separation Wall, constructed in the early 2000s, physically divided Christian communities from their lands and each other, creating a network of walls and checkpoints that made daily life an ordeal.

The consequences of these actions have been profound. Christian communities have been reduced to small enclaves, surrounded by Israeli settlements and military installations. The once-vibrant Christian populations of towns like Bethlehem have shrunk dramatically, with many families choosing to emigrate rather than live under the constant strain of occupation. Churches and monasteries that have stood for centuries now find themselves isolated, surrounded by walls and checkpoints that restrict access to worshippers and pilgrims. In some cases, church-owned lands have been targeted for confiscation, either through legal loopholes or outright land grabs by settlers, further eroding the presence of Christianity in the region.

Military actions by Israel have also played a significant role in displacing Christian populations. During both the 1948 war and the Six-Day War in 1967, Israeli military campaigns resulted in the destruction of Christian homes, churches, and businesses. In 1967, when Israel captured East Jerusalem, the West Bank, and Gaza, the occupation intensified. Christians, like their Muslim neighbors, found themselves under military rule, subject to restrictions on movement, employment, and political expression. In the years since, military incursions and clashes between Israeli forces and Palestinians have further destabilized Christian communities, particularly in areas like Gaza, where Christian families are trapped between the harsh realities of Israeli blockades and internal political turmoil.

The ongoing confiscation of land, the expansion of settlements, and the military occupation have all combined to systematically erode the Christian presence in the Holy Land. What was once a diverse and vibrant Christian community has been reduced to a fraction of its original size. The loss of land, in particular, has had a devastating impact on the economic and cultural survival of Palestinian Christians. Without access to their ancestral lands, many families have lost their primary means of livelihood. Churches, too, have suffered, as their congregations dwindle and their lands are encroached upon by settlers.

The impact of Israeli control is not only felt in the physical displacement of Christian communities but also in the psychological and spiritual toll it has taken. For many Palestinian Christians, the Holy Land is more than just a place of religious significance—it is their home, the land where their ancestors lived, worshipped, and built a future for their families. The slow but steady erasure of Christian communities from this land is a deep wound that cuts to the heart of their identity.

As Israeli policies continue to prioritize the expansion of Jewish settlements and the consolidation of land, the future of Palestinian Christians in the Holy Land grows increasingly uncertain. The displacement of Christian communities and the seizure of their lands is not just a historical event; it is an ongoing process, one that threatens to erase a 2,000-year-old presence in the land where Christianity was born. For the Christians of Palestine, the impact of Israeli control is felt every day, in the loss of their homes, their churches, and their connection to the land that holds the deepest meaning for their faith.

Chapter 2: Churches Under Siege: The Struggle for Survival in Occupied Palestine

In the Holy Land, where some of Christianity's most sacred sites are located, the very churches that have stood as symbols of faith and endurance for centuries are now under siege. The ongoing Israeli occupation has not only disrupted the lives of Palestinian Christians but has also directly impacted the churches that serve as the heart of their religious and community life. From the Church of the Nativity in Bethlehem to the Church of the Holy Sepulchre in Jerusalem, these holy sites are not merely historical landmarks; they are active places of worship and pilgrimage. Yet, for many Christians, access to these sites has become a daily struggle, restricted by Israeli military control, checkpoints, and the encroachment of Jewish settlers.

Israeli military control over the West Bank and East Jerusalem has severely limited the freedom of movement for Palestinian Christians, making it increasingly difficult to visit their most revered holy sites. For Christians in Bethlehem, for example, attending services at the Church of the Holy Sepulchre in Jerusalem requires passing through a network of military checkpoints and obtaining special permits, which are often difficult to secure. The Separation Wall, which divides much of the West Bank from Jerusalem, physically isolates Christian communities from these sacred places, turning what should be a simple act of worship into a complex and often humiliating process. Pilgrims from abroad may come and go with relative ease, but for the Christians who live in Palestine, access to their holiest places is far from guaranteed.

The Church of the Nativity, traditionally believed to be the birthplace of Jesus Christ, is one such site that has been heavily affected by the occupation. Located in Bethlehem, the church is now surrounded by Israeli military checkpoints and walls, cutting it off from Jerusalem and other parts of the West Bank. While it remains a popular destination for international pilgrims, local Christians face increasing difficulties in visiting the site due to the numerous restrictions imposed by Israeli authorities. The same holds true for the Church of the Holy Sepulchre in Jerusalem, which marks the site of Christ's crucifixion and resurrection. Although it is one of the most important pilgrimage sites for Christians worldwide, Palestinian Christians from the West Bank and Gaza face numerous barriers in reaching the church, with access often granted only during specific religious holidays or for brief periods.

The situation is exacerbated by the fact that church-owned lands have also come under threat from Israeli authorities and Jewish settlers. Through legal loopholes and forceful measures, land that has been owned and maintained by churches for centuries is being slowly eroded. Jewish settlers, backed by the Israeli government, have increasingly encroached on land owned by Christian institutions, particularly in areas surrounding key holy sites. Churches and monasteries have faced legal battles over property rights, often losing their land through dubious legal rulings that favor settlers. The Israeli government has used the Absentee Property Law to confiscate church-owned lands, particularly those of Christian communities that were displaced during the 1948 war. As a result, churches have not only lost vital land but have also seen their ability to serve their congregations severely diminished.

One particularly notable case is the situation of the Cremisan Valley, near Bethlehem, where land owned by the Catholic Church has been threatened by the construction of the Israeli Separation Wall. For years, the church and local Christian families have fought legal battles to prevent the confiscation of this land, which includes vineyards used by the church and a monastery. Despite international outcry, Israeli authorities have continued to push for the wall's construction, which would cut off the monastery and isolate the Christian community in the area. This is just one of many examples of how Israeli policies have targeted church lands, weakening the church's ability to function as a place of worship and refuge.

The churches in Palestine are not only facing physical encroachment on their land but are also struggling to survive in a climate of constant surveillance and restriction. Under Israeli occupation, church activities are closely monitored, and religious leaders must navigate a complex web of permits and regulations to carry out even basic functions. Priests and church workers are often subject to travel restrictions, making it difficult to attend to the needs of their congregations. The Israeli government has also imposed limitations on the ability of churches to bring in foreign clergy, further straining their ability to operate. In addition, the economic hardships faced by Palestinian Christians, compounded by the occupation, have left many churches without the financial resources needed to maintain their buildings or provide essential services to their communities.

International support for these churches has also been stifled by Israeli restrictions. Many Christian organizations from abroad that seek to provide aid or assistance to Palestinian churches face bureaucratic obstacles and are often denied entry or permits by the Israeli government. This isolation has left Palestinian churches increasingly cut off from the global Christian community, further weakening their ability to sustain their presence in the Holy Land. Without international solidarity and support, these churches are left to struggle alone against the overwhelming pressures of occupation and land seizure.

The ongoing suppression of churches in Palestine is not just a matter of political control; it is an attack on the spiritual and cultural heart of Palestinian Christianity. As churches lose land, face restrictions, and struggle to access their own holy sites, the very survival of Christianity in the land where it was born is at risk. These churches are more than just buildings; they are the lifeblood of the Christian community, places where faith, culture, and history intersect. Yet, under Israeli occupation, they are being systematically dismantled, piece by piece.

The story of the churches under siege in Palestine is one of resilience in the face of overwhelming odds. Despite the constant challenges, these institutions continue to serve their communities, offering not just spiritual guidance but also education, healthcare, and social services. However, their future is uncertain. The ongoing Israeli occupation, coupled with the increasing encroachment of settlers, threatens to erase the Christian presence in the Holy Land, leaving behind only the physical remnants of a once-thriving religious tradition. The struggle for the survival of these churches is, in many ways, the struggle for the survival of Christianity itself in its birthplace.

Restricted Access to Holy Sites: A Barrier to Faith

FOR PALESTINIAN CHRISTIANS, the sacred act of visiting their holiest sites—places that have been at the center of their faith for centuries—has become an increasingly difficult and frustrating ordeal. Israeli military control over the West Bank and East Jerusalem has drastically limited access to these revered places of worship, particularly for those living in Palestinian territories. The Church of the Nativity in Bethlehem and the Church of the Holy Sepulchre in Jerusalem are two of the most important sites for Christians worldwide, marking the birth and resurrection of Jesus Christ. Yet, for the Christians living in the very land where these sacred events took place, simply visiting these holy sites can feel like an impossible challenge.

The Separation Wall, built by Israel in the early 2000s, serves as a physical and symbolic barrier that separates Palestinian Christians from the places most central to their faith. The Wall cuts through the West Bank, enclosing Bethlehem, and making movement between the city and Jerusalem an arduous task. While international pilgrims can visit the Church of the Nativity with relative ease, local Palestinian Christians are forced to navigate a network of military checkpoints, security screenings, and permit systems that often deny or delay their access. What should be a simple pilgrimage or act of worship becomes a prolonged and humiliating experience, one that deters many from even attempting the journey.

For the Christians of Bethlehem, attending religious services or major festivals at the Church of the Holy Sepulchre in Jerusalem is particularly fraught. Situated in the heart of the Old City, this church holds profound significance as the site of Christ's crucifixion, burial, and resurrection. But for Palestinians living in the West Bank, visiting the church often requires special permits issued by Israeli authorities. These permits are difficult to obtain, and even when granted, they are often valid for only short periods, typically around major Christian holidays such as Easter or Christmas. Many Christians, especially young people, are denied permits entirely, or forced to wait through long, uncertain application processes. This severely restricts their ability to freely practice their faith, as their access to one of Christianity's holiest places is tightly controlled by a government that limits their movement.

The same limitations apply to access to the Church of the Nativity, the traditional site of Christ's birth, which sits in the heart of Bethlehem, now surrounded by the Separation Wall and military checkpoints. Though international pilgrims continue to visit the site in large numbers, Palestinian Christians must pass through numerous military barriers to reach this church, which is just a few miles from Jerusalem but feels worlds away due to the barriers that isolate the city. These restrictions are especially painful for Christians during significant religious periods, such as Christmas and Easter, when access to holy sites should be a central part of their religious life and celebrations.

Even during major religious events, such as Easter processions in Jerusalem, Christians from the West Bank and Gaza face immense obstacles. Israeli forces often limit the number of permits issued for these events, drastically reducing the number of Palestinians who can participate. Even those who do receive permits often find themselves subject to heavy surveillance and military control, with soldiers and police monitoring their movements as they attempt to reach their holy sites. The sense of oppression is palpable; the sacred act of pilgrimage becomes a battle against bureaucracy and militarization.

These barriers to holy sites are not just about physical access—they also represent a broader form of spiritual and cultural isolation for Palestinian Christians. The difficulty in reaching these sacred places erodes their connection to the physical manifestations of their faith, cutting them off from the places where they have worshipped for centuries. For many, the inability to freely visit and pray at these sites deepens the sense of loss and alienation they feel living under occupation. The holy sites are not just historical relics; they are living, breathing parts of Christian faith and identity, and the restrictions placed on access are an attack on that identity.

Moreover, the economic impact of these restrictions is felt by the broader Christian community in Palestine. Holy sites like the Church of the Nativity and the Church of the Holy Sepulchre are not just places of worship—they are central to the tourism industry that sustains many Christian families and businesses in cities like Bethlehem and Jerusalem. The Israeli military control, combined with frequent closures and restricted access, has hurt these local economies, cutting off vital sources of income for families who depend on pilgrimage tourism.

Despite these challenges, Palestinian Christians continue to hold on to their faith, finding ways to celebrate and worship even under such oppressive conditions. Churches and communities organize alternative prayer gatherings when access to holy sites is restricted, and during festivals like Christmas and Easter, they come together to express their solidarity and commitment to maintaining their religious traditions. However, the strain is undeniable, and the ability to freely practice their faith in the land where Christianity was born is increasingly under threat.

The restrictions placed on access to these holy sites are a constant reminder of the broader reality of occupation for Palestinian Christians. The physical barriers, military checkpoints, and bureaucratic hurdles symbolize the deeper struggle to maintain their presence in the Holy Land. As the occupation continues, the sacred sites that have long been a source of spiritual sustenance for Palestinian Christians are becoming increasingly out of reach, leaving them isolated not only from the land but from their own faith.

Church Land Confiscation: The Encroachment on Sacred Ground

THROUGHOUT THE HOLY Land, the confiscation of church-owned lands has become a symbol of the broader struggle faced by Palestinian Christians under Israeli occupation. Over the years, Israeli authorities and Jewish settlers have systematically encroached upon church properties, using a combination of legal loopholes, bureaucratic manipulation, and outright force to seize land that has been in the hands of Christian communities for centuries. These lands, which have served not only as places of worship but also as agricultural, educational, and communal centers, are now under constant threat. This land confiscation has severely undermined the ability of churches to serve their congregations and has contributed to the broader erosion of Christian life in Palestine.

One of the key tools used by Israel to confiscate church land is the Absentee Property Law, enacted in 1950. This law allows the Israeli government to take possession of properties owned by Palestinians, including Christians, who were displaced during the 1948 war or who were not physically present when the land was registered. Under this law, many Christian families and religious institutions lost vast amounts of land, which were transferred to Israeli authorities or sold to Jewish settlers. This legal mechanism has been a cornerstone of the Israeli state's effort to claim more territory, particularly in areas surrounding Jerusalem, Bethlehem, and other historically Christian regions.

In addition to the Absentee Property Law, other legal loopholes have been exploited to target church-owned lands. For example, in cases where churches have leased land to Palestinian families or businesses, Israeli courts have allowed settlers to claim ownership of these properties under dubious legal grounds. This has been particularly common in East Jerusalem, where Jewish settler organizations have aggressively pursued claims against church-owned lands, often backed by powerful political and financial forces. Settler groups, with the tacit approval of the Israeli government, have taken over properties belonging to churches, using court rulings and under-the-table deals to secure land that has been held by Christian institutions for generations.

A prime example of this encroachment is the case of the Greek Orthodox Church, which has been embroiled in multiple legal battles over its properties in Jerusalem. In recent years, it was revealed that key properties owned by the church, including land in the Old City near the Jaffa Gate, had been secretly sold to Jewish settler organizations. These sales, carried out under questionable circumstances, have sparked outrage among Palestinian Christians, who view them as part of a broader effort to push out Christian communities from the city's most important religious and historical areas. Despite protests and legal challenges, these properties have largely fallen into the hands of settlers, further eroding the Christian presence in one of the faith's most sacred cities.

The ongoing confiscation of church land is not limited to Jerusalem. In the Cremisan Valley near Bethlehem, the Catholic Church has faced a prolonged battle to protect its lands from Israeli confiscation. The Cremisan Monastery and its surrounding vineyards, which have provided livelihood and sanctuary for the local Christian community, were targeted by the Israeli government as part of the construction of the Separation Wall. Despite international condemnation and appeals from the Vatican, sections of the church's land were seized, and the wall now cuts through what was once church property, separating the monastery from the local community. This is just one example of how Israeli infrastructure projects, such as the construction of the wall and the expansion of settlements, have led to the confiscation of church lands.

Jewish settlers have also taken more aggressive, forceful measures to claim church-owned land. In some cases, settlers have physically occupied church properties, setting up outposts or taking over buildings, often with little to no interference from Israeli authorities. These illegal settlements are frequently established on land owned by Christian churches, particularly in the West Bank, where settlers have increasingly targeted lands owned by monasteries and other religious institutions. The lack of legal recourse for churches, coupled with the Israeli government's unwillingness to intervene, has allowed these settlers to remain on church property, further entrenching the occupation of Christian lands.

The consequences of these land confiscations have been profound. Churches, which have long been central to the social, spiritual, and economic life of Palestinian Christian communities, are being stripped of their ability to function effectively. Without their land, churches cannot sustain their agricultural projects, which provide income and food for local communities. Monasteries and convents, which rely on their surrounding lands for seclusion and self-sufficiency, are increasingly encroached upon, disrupting the lives of the religious orders that inhabit them. Schools, hospitals, and other church-run institutions have also been affected, as the loss of land reduces their capacity to serve the broader community.

The erosion of church-owned lands is not just an economic or legal issue; it is a spiritual and cultural one. For Palestinian Christians, the land is deeply intertwined with their identity and their faith. The churches and monasteries that dot the landscape of Palestine are not merely buildings—they are living institutions that connect the present generation of Christians to their ancestors and to the very roots of their faith. The confiscation of these lands threatens to sever that connection, pushing Christian communities further to the margins and weakening their presence in the Holy Land.

Despite the ongoing confiscations, Palestinian Christians and their religious leaders continue to resist. Churches have launched legal challenges, organized protests, and appealed to the international community for support in their fight to retain their land. However, the legal and political landscape is overwhelmingly stacked against them, and the encroachment on church property continues. The loss of church-owned lands is part of a broader strategy of displacement that has targeted Palestinian communities for decades, and as long as these policies persist, the future of Christianity in the land where it was born remains at risk.

This systematic seizure of church land is not just about control of territory—it is an assault on the very existence of Palestinian Christians and their ability to maintain their religious and cultural heritage. As churches lose their land, they lose their ability to support their congregations, to serve their communities, and to provide a place of worship in a land increasingly dominated by settlers and military occupation. The battle for church land is, in many ways, the battle for the survival of Christianity in the Holy Land.

Churches Struggling to Survive: The Daily Challenges of Occupation

THE CHURCHES OF PALESTINE, once central to the lives of local Christian communities, are now struggling to survive under the weight of Israeli occupation. These institutions, which have long served as places of worship, education, and social support, face constant challenges that hinder their ability to function as they once did. The pressures of military occupation, with its surveillance, movement restrictions, and bureaucratic obstacles, have made it nearly impossible for churches to operate freely. Combined with a lack of access to international support due to Israeli control, Palestinian churches find themselves isolated, weakened, and on the brink of collapse.

One of the most immediate challenges faced by churches in Palestine is the pervasive presence of Israeli military surveillance. Church activities, from religious services to community events, are closely monitored by Israeli authorities, especially in areas like Jerusalem and Bethlehem. Security forces routinely monitor gatherings, often creating a sense of fear and unease among worshippers. This constant surveillance is not only intrusive but also undermines the sacredness of church spaces, turning places of prayer into locations of suspicion and control. Religious leaders, too, are subject to this scrutiny, with their movements and activities often restricted or heavily scrutinized by military authorities.

The Israeli system of checkpoints, permits, and travel restrictions further complicates the ability of churches to serve their congregations. Priests and church workers frequently face difficulties in moving between cities and regions, often needing special permits to travel to different parishes or to attend religious events. The process of obtaining these permits is fraught with bureaucratic delays and arbitrary denials, making it difficult for religious leaders to carry out their pastoral duties. For many priests, simply traveling from Bethlehem to Jerusalem—a journey of a few miles—requires passing through military checkpoints, where they may be detained, questioned, or turned back. These restrictions not only limit the ability of church leaders to minister to their communities but also disrupt the spiritual life of the people they serve.

The restrictions on movement extend to the congregations themselves. Many Palestinian Christians are unable to attend church services regularly, particularly in areas like East Jerusalem, where permits are required to enter the city. This has had a devastating effect on church attendance, with many congregations shrinking as a result. Festivals and religious celebrations, which once brought entire communities together, are now marked by the absence of many who are prevented from attending due to military restrictions. The spiritual and emotional toll of this isolation is profound, as churches, which have long been centers of communal life, are increasingly empty and disconnected from their congregants.

In addition to these restrictions, churches face significant financial difficulties, exacerbated by the broader economic challenges of life under occupation. Many church-run institutions, such as schools, hospitals, and charities, rely on donations and international support to operate. However, the Israeli occupation has made it increasingly difficult for these churches to access the international aid they once relied on. International organizations seeking to support Palestinian churches often face bureaucratic obstacles, including delays in permits, restrictions on the transfer of funds, and barriers to shipping supplies. The Israeli government's tight control over borders and entry points has severely limited the ability of churches to receive the help they need from the global Christian community.

The economic strain is particularly acute for churches that own agricultural land or other sources of income. As Israeli settlements expand and land is confiscated, churches are losing the resources that once sustained them. Many monasteries and convents, which traditionally relied on farming or other small industries to support their work, are now cut off from their lands, either by the Separation Wall or by settler encroachment. Without these resources, churches struggle to pay their staff, maintain their buildings, or provide essential services to their communities. The loss of income has also forced some churches to reduce or close their charitable programs, which have long been a vital source of support for the most vulnerable members of Palestinian society.

The isolation of Palestinian churches is compounded by the lack of international visibility and support. While global Christian organizations and churches have often expressed solidarity with Palestinian Christians, their efforts are frequently stymied by the realities of Israeli control. Foreign clergy, volunteers, and aid workers face significant challenges in obtaining visas or permits to work in Palestine, and those who do manage to enter the region are often restricted in their movements. This isolation has left Palestinian churches increasingly cut off from the global Christian community, further weakening their ability to function and survive.

Despite these overwhelming challenges, Palestinian churches continue to persevere, driven by their deep-rooted faith and commitment to their communities. Religious leaders and church workers, despite the constant surveillance and restrictions, remain dedicated to their mission of serving their congregations. Churches continue to provide education, healthcare, and social services, even as their resources dwindle and their activities are curtailed by the occupation. However, the future of these institutions remains uncertain. As the occupation continues and the pressures on churches mount, the very survival of Christianity in the Holy Land is at risk.

The struggle of Palestinian churches is not just a struggle for religious freedom; it is a struggle for survival in the face of systemic oppression. These institutions, which have stood as pillars of the Christian community for centuries, are now being dismantled, piece by piece, by the realities of occupation. Without international support and intervention, the churches of Palestine may soon find themselves unable to continue their vital work, leaving the Christian community even more vulnerable and isolated in the land where their faith was born. The story of these churches is one of resilience in the face of immense adversity, but without a change in the conditions of occupation, their struggle may ultimately lead to their erasure from the Holy Land.

Chapter 3: Israeli Laws and Policies That Oppress Christians

For Palestinian Christians, life under Israeli control is defined by a complex web of laws and policies that systematically erode their rights, their access to land, and their ability to maintain a stable and sustainable community. While the broader conflict between Israelis and Palestinians is often framed in terms of Jewish-Muslim relations, Palestinian Christians are equally affected by the legal and political structures imposed by the Israeli government. These laws and policies, though often presented as necessary for security or administrative reasons, have had a devastating impact on the Christian community, undermining their presence in the Holy Land and threatening their future.

One of the most powerful tools of oppression used by the Israeli state is land confiscation, particularly through the implementation of the Absentee Property Law. This law, enacted in 1950, allows the Israeli government to take ownership of properties owned by Palestinians who were displaced during the 1948 war, categorizing them as "absentees." This law has been used extensively to seize lands belonging to Palestinian Christians, many of whom fled during times of conflict or were unable to maintain continuous presence on their property due to restrictions. Under this legal framework, Christian families and church institutions have lost vast amounts of land, which have been transferred to Israeli state ownership or sold to Jewish settlers. For many Christian communities, this confiscation of land is not just a material loss—it is a profound violation of their connection to their ancestral homes and places of worship.

The expansion of Jewish settlements on these confiscated lands has further marginalized Christian communities. Settlements, often supported by the Israeli government, have encroached on areas that were once home to Christian families and institutions, particularly in places like Bethlehem and the surrounding villages. The presence of these settlements has not only taken land from Christians but has also introduced new layers of restriction and surveillance, as military checkpoints and security zones are established to protect settlers. This expansion has fractured Christian communities, cutting them off from each other and limiting their ability to live, work, and worship freely.

The construction of the Separation Wall has been another key factor in the oppression of Palestinian Christians. Ostensibly built for security reasons, the wall has had a profound impact on Christian life in the West Bank. It physically divides communities, separating families and cutting off access to vital services like education, healthcare, and employment. For many Christian families, the wall represents not just a physical barrier but also a spiritual one, as it isolates them from their churches and religious sites. In Bethlehem, for example, the wall cuts through the town, making it difficult for Christians to travel to Jerusalem for worship or to visit family members on the other side of the barrier. This division has had a particularly harsh effect on Christian youth, who find their opportunities for education and employment limited by their inability to move freely between cities.

The wall has also significantly reduced access to holy sites, which are central to the spiritual and communal life of Palestinian Christians. Many Christians are now required to obtain special permits to visit places like the Church of the Holy Sepulchre in Jerusalem or the Church of the Nativity in Bethlehem. These permits are difficult to obtain, and even when granted, they are often temporary or restricted to certain religious holidays. This restriction has eroded the connection that Palestinian Christians have to their most sacred sites, creating a sense of isolation and alienation from the physical manifestations of their faith.

Discriminatory zoning and building laws further complicate the survival of Christian institutions in the Holy Land. Israeli zoning laws in Jerusalem and the West Bank severely limit the ability of Christian churches and organizations to expand or restore their buildings. Churches seeking to renovate or add new structures often face years of bureaucratic delays, legal challenges, and outright denials. In many cases, these restrictions have forced churches into a state of decline, as they are unable to maintain their aging buildings or provide adequate facilities for their congregations. The difficulty in obtaining permits for construction or expansion is not limited to churches; schools, hospitals, and other church-run institutions face similar challenges. These institutions, which have long provided vital services to both Christians and Muslims in Palestine, are being starved of the resources they need to continue functioning.

The struggle to retain residency rights is another significant challenge faced by Palestinian Christians, particularly in Jerusalem. Israeli laws governing residency are designed to make it difficult for Palestinians to maintain a permanent presence in the city. One of the most problematic laws is the revocation of residency rights for those who live outside the city for extended periods. This law disproportionately affects Christians, many of whom have been forced to leave Jerusalem temporarily due to economic hardship, education, or family reasons. Upon returning, they often find that their residency rights have been revoked, making it nearly impossible for them to live or work legally in the city. This policy has led to a steady decline in the Christian population of Jerusalem, as more and more families are forced to leave permanently.

The combination of land confiscation, settlement expansion, the Separation Wall, discriminatory building laws, and residency struggles has created an environment of systemic oppression for Palestinian Christians. These policies are not isolated incidents; they are part of a broader strategy to marginalize Palestinian communities—Christian and Muslim alike—and to secure greater control over the land. For the Christian community, which is already a small minority, these legal and political pressures have had a devastating effect, pushing many to emigrate in search of greater freedom and stability elsewhere.

As these laws and policies continue to tighten their grip on the daily lives of Palestinian Christians, the future of Christianity in the Holy Land becomes increasingly uncertain. The very institutions that have sustained Christian life for centuries—churches, schools, and hospitals—are under threat, while the Christian community itself faces the prospect of becoming an even smaller and more marginalized minority in the land of its origin. Without significant changes to these laws and policies, the Christian presence in Palestine may one day become little more than a memory, a relic of a time when the Holy Land was a place of diverse religious and cultural coexistence.

Land Confiscation and Settlement Expansion: The Erosion of Christian-Owned Lands

FOR PALESTINIAN CHRISTIANS, land is more than just property—it is a vital connection to their history, their community, and their identity. For centuries, Christian families and church institutions have owned and maintained significant portions of land in Palestine, using it for farming, housing, education, and worship. However, since the establishment of the state of Israel, these lands have come under increasing threat from Israeli laws and policies designed to confiscate property and facilitate the expansion of Jewish settlements. One of the most powerful tools in this process has been the Absentee Property Law, which has systematically stripped Palestinian Christians of their land, furthering the displacement of their communities.

The Absentee Property Law, enacted by Israel in 1950, allows the state to confiscate land belonging to Palestinians who were displaced during the 1948 Arab-Israeli war. Under this law, any Palestinian who fled their home—either within Palestine or to neighboring countries—was classified as an "absentee," and their property was transferred to the Israeli Custodian of Absentee Property. This law disproportionately affected Christians, many of whom were forced to flee during the war, seeking refuge in Jordan, Lebanon, or other nearby areas. Despite the fact that many of these Christian families had lived on their land for generations, their absence during the war gave the Israeli state the legal pretext to seize their properties, which were then sold or transferred to Jewish settlers.

The impact of the Absentee Property Law on Christian-owned land has been profound. In areas like Jerusalem, Bethlehem, and the surrounding villages, Christian families lost large tracts of land, including homes, farms, and businesses. Much of this land has since been developed into Jewish settlements, further eroding the Christian presence in these historically significant regions. For the Christian community, the loss of land is not just a material loss—it is a spiritual and cultural wound, as land ownership is deeply tied to their identity and their connection to the land where their faith was born.

In addition to the Absentee Property Law, other legal mechanisms have been used to confiscate Christian-owned land. Israeli authorities have employed a range of policies that exploit legal ambiguities, bureaucratic hurdles, and zoning restrictions to seize land from Palestinian Christians. One such method is the use of expropriation for public use, where land is taken under the pretext of security or infrastructure projects, such as the construction of roads, military installations, or the Separation Wall. While these projects are often framed as necessary for the safety of Israeli citizens, the reality is that they disproportionately affect Palestinian landowners, including

Christians, and often serve as a means to expand Israeli control over Palestinian territories.

The expansion of Jewish settlements in the West Bank and East Jerusalem has further exacerbated the problem. Settlement construction, which is actively supported by the Israeli government, often encroaches on land owned by Christian families and religious institutions. In many cases, settlers have built homes, outposts, or agricultural developments on land that legally belongs to Christian churches or individuals, with little to no intervention from Israeli authorities. Even when legal challenges are brought against these settlers, the Israeli court system rarely rules in favor of Palestinian landowners, effectively sanctioning the continued encroachment on Christian property.

One particularly egregious example of this encroachment is the situation in Beit Jala, a predominantly Christian town near Bethlehem. In this area, Jewish settlers have expanded onto land that belongs to local Christian families and the Catholic Church, using legal loopholes and government backing to claim ownership. The construction of the Separation Wall in this region has also cut off Christian families from their land, as the wall snakes through the area, isolating homes and farms from their owners. Despite protests and legal battles, the expansion of settlements continues, gradually erasing the presence of Christians in the region.

The impact of land confiscation and settlement expansion on Christian communities cannot be overstated. Land is not just an economic asset for these families—it is their heritage, their livelihood, and their connection to the Holy Land. The loss of land has driven many Christians to emigrate, seeking better opportunities abroad as they face the reality that they can no longer live or work on the land their families have owned for generations. This has led to a steady decline in the Christian population of Palestine, as those who remain struggle to hold on to what little land they still possess.

For the churches, the loss of land is equally devastating. Church-owned lands have historically been used to support a variety of community functions, from monasteries and schools to agricultural projects that provide food and income for local Christians. As these lands are confiscated or encroached upon by settlers, churches are left with fewer resources to sustain their religious and social missions. In some cases, entire parcels of church land have been taken over by settlers, who build outposts or homes with impunity, knowing that the legal system is unlikely to force them to leave.

The ongoing confiscation of Christian-owned land is not just a byproduct of the Israeli-Palestinian conflict—it is a deliberate strategy to weaken the Palestinian presence, including Christians, in the Holy Land. By seizing land and allowing settlements to expand, the Israeli government is ensuring that the Christian community remains a marginalized and shrinking minority. The loss of land not only threatens the economic and social stability of Palestinian Christians but also undermines their ability to maintain their cultural and religious heritage in the place where Christianity was born.

As settlement expansion continues and legal frameworks like the Absentee Property Law remain in place, the future of Christian land ownership in Palestine grows increasingly uncertain. The erosion of Christian-owned lands is part of a broader pattern of displacement and dispossession that has characterized life for Palestinians under Israeli occupation. For the Christian community, which is already a small minority, the loss of land represents an existential threat to their continued presence in the land they have called home for centuries.

The Separation Wall: Dividing Christian Communities and Shattering Daily Life

THE CONSTRUCTION OF the Israeli Separation Wall has become one of the most visible symbols of the occupation, profoundly affecting the lives of Palestinians, including the Christian communities of the West Bank. Built ostensibly for security purposes, the Wall has had far-reaching consequences for Christian families, churches, schools, and livelihoods. The Wall physically divides communities, restricts access to religious and educational institutions, and severely limits economic opportunities. For Palestinian Christians, the Separation Wall represents not only a physical barrier but also a psychological and spiritual separation from their land, their holy sites, and each other.

The Wall, which stretches over 700 kilometers, cuts through Palestinian towns and villages, enclosing areas like Bethlehem, Beit Jala, and Beit Sahour, which have long been home to significant Christian populations. For these communities, the construction of the Wall has meant the loss of land, homes, and the freedom of movement. Christian families find themselves isolated from their relatives and neighbors, as the Wall separates homes from schools, churches, and workplaces. In Bethlehem, the birthplace of Jesus Christ, the Wall looms over the town, severing the community from Jerusalem and other key cities, making it nearly impossible for Christians to visit holy sites like the Church of the Holy Sepulchre in the Old City.

The impact of the Wall on Christian religious life is profound. For many Palestinian Christians, regular worship at their most sacred sites has become a difficult, if not impossible, task. The Wall's checkpoints and permit systems restrict movement, requiring Christians to apply for special permits to visit places of worship, particularly in Jerusalem. Even on important religious holidays such as Christmas and Easter, when Christians would traditionally make pilgrimages to these holy sites, access is often denied or heavily limited. The spiritual and emotional toll of being cut off from these sacred places is immense, as the Wall symbolizes a forced separation from the physical manifestations of their faith.

For the Church of the Nativity in Bethlehem, a site of immense significance as the traditional birthplace of Jesus, the Wall has isolated the town from much of the West Bank and Jerusalem, turning it into a virtual prison. While international tourists and pilgrims can access the church, local Palestinian Christians face roadblocks and military checkpoints just to attend services. The Wall has also restricted the flow of visitors and pilgrims to Bethlehem, devastating the local economy, which has long relied on tourism linked to the church. The once vibrant Christian community of Bethlehem now finds itself struggling economically, with many families considering emigration as their only option for survival.

Schools and educational institutions run by Christian churches and organizations have also been deeply affected by the Wall. Many Christian children must pass through checkpoints daily to reach their schools, enduring long waits and often unpredictable delays. The psychological stress of living behind the Wall, combined with the difficulties of accessing basic education, has had a demoralizing effect on Palestinian Christian youth. In some cases, families have been forced to move closer to these institutions to avoid the daily ordeal of crossing the Wall, but this often means leaving behind their homes, extended families, and agricultural lands.

The Separation Wall has not only disrupted access to education and worship but has also devastated the economic livelihoods of Christian families. For many, agriculture has been a primary source of income, but the Wall has cut off farmers from their land, making it nearly impossible to tend to their crops or harvest their produce. Olive groves, vineyards, and farmlands that have been passed down through generations are now inaccessible, trapped behind the Wall or lost to expanding settlements. The economic consequences of this are dire, as families lose their main sources of income and are forced into poverty. The Wall has also cut off access to markets, further limiting the ability of Palestinian Christians to sell their goods or trade with neighboring communities.

The psychological effects of the Wall on Christian communities are equally damaging. The sense of isolation, both physically and spiritually, has led to a growing sense of despair and hopelessness among many Palestinian Christians. Families are separated, their movement is restricted, and their access to places of worship and education is severely limited. The Wall has created a divide not only between Palestinians and Israelis but also within Palestinian society itself, fragmenting communities and making daily life a struggle for survival. For many Christians, the Wall represents a form of collective punishment, stripping them of their dignity and their ability to live freely in the land where their faith was born.

Despite these challenges, Palestinian Christians continue to show resilience in the face of the Wall's oppressive presence. Churches and religious leaders work tirelessly to maintain their communities, providing spiritual support and social services to those affected by the Wall's restrictions. Local organizations, often supported by international Christian networks, have stepped in to offer educational programs, legal assistance, and economic aid to help families cope with the hardships imposed by the Wall. However, the future remains uncertain. As long as the Wall stands, the Christian community in Palestine will remain divided, with their ability to thrive and practice their faith severely compromised.

The Separation Wall has become a lasting symbol of division and oppression for Palestinian Christians. Its construction has not only limited their access to the churches, schools, and livelihoods that sustain their communities but has also deepened their sense of isolation from the world and their own faith. For a community already struggling to maintain its presence in the Holy Land, the Wall is a constant reminder of their marginalization and the uncertainty of their future in the land of their ancestors.

Discriminatory Zoning and Building Laws:

Hindering the Growth of Christian Institutions

IN ADDITION TO THE physical barriers created by the Separation Wall and the ongoing settlement expansion, Israeli zoning and building laws have imposed another set of challenges for Palestinian Christian communities. These laws, often discriminatory in nature, make it extremely difficult for Christian churches, schools, and other community buildings to expand, renovate, or even maintain their current structures. By restricting building permits and enforcing strict zoning regulations, Israeli authorities have created an environment in which Christian institutions are forced into gradual decline, struggling to sustain themselves in a land where they have historically thrived.

One of the primary obstacles faced by Christian communities is the Israeli government's control over land-use policies in both East Jerusalem and the West Bank. Under Israeli zoning laws, large portions of these areas are designated as "green zones" or "military zones," where building is either heavily restricted or entirely prohibited. This zoning strategy often targets Palestinian areas, including those inhabited by Christians, effectively preventing any new construction or development. Even in areas where building is technically allowed, the process of obtaining permits is mired in bureaucracy, with applications often delayed for years or outright denied without explanation.

For Christian churches and institutions, these zoning laws have been particularly damaging. Churches seeking to expand their facilities to accommodate growing congregations or to renovate aging buildings face an uphill battle in securing the necessary permits. In many cases, churches are forced to wait years for approval, only to have their applications rejected based on arbitrary technicalities. This has left many churches in a state of disrepair, unable to make even basic improvements to their buildings. Over time, this lack of maintenance weakens the physical infrastructure of these institutions, diminishing their ability to serve their communities.

The difficulties faced by Christian institutions in obtaining building permits are not limited to churches alone. Schools, hospitals, and other community facilities operated by Christian organizations are subject to the same discriminatory practices. Many Christian schools, which provide vital education to both Christian and Muslim students, are unable to expand their campuses or build new classrooms to meet the needs of their students. Similarly, Christian hospitals and clinics, which have historically served both Palestinian and Israeli populations, struggle to maintain their facilities due to the near impossibility of obtaining permits for expansion or renovation.

These zoning restrictions are not just an administrative hurdle—they are part of a broader strategy to limit the growth and sustainability of Christian communities in the Holy Land. By restricting the ability of churches and institutions to expand, Israeli authorities are effectively forcing these communities into stagnation. As buildings fall into disrepair and congregations outgrow their facilities, the long-term viability of Christian institutions becomes increasingly uncertain. For a community already facing economic and social pressures, these building restrictions add yet another layer of difficulty, making it harder for Christians to maintain their presence in the land where their faith was born.

One of the most troubling aspects of these discriminatory zoning laws is the contrast between the restrictions placed on Christian communities and the freedom granted to Israeli settlers. In areas where Christian churches are struggling to obtain building permits, Jewish settlements are rapidly expanding, often with full government support. New homes, schools, and community centers are built for settlers on land that was once owned by Palestinian Christians, while the churches and institutions that have existed for centuries are denied the basic right to grow. This unequal treatment highlights the political motivations behind the zoning laws, which prioritize the expansion of Jewish settlements at the expense of Palestinian communities, including Christians.

In some cases, Christian churches and organizations have been forced to carry out renovations or expansions without the proper permits, simply because the official process is so restrictive and unyielding. However, this comes with great risk, as Israeli authorities frequently issue demolition orders for buildings constructed without permits. In East Jerusalem and the West Bank, churches, schools, and homes that have been built or expanded without official approval are often targeted for demolition, leaving Christian communities with little recourse. The threat of demolition hangs over many Christian institutions, further discouraging any attempts at growth or development.

The long-term effects of these discriminatory zoning and building laws are deeply concerning for the future of Palestinian Christian communities. As churches, schools, and hospitals fall into disrepair and struggle to serve their congregations, many Christians are left with little choice but to emigrate in search of better opportunities. This steady emigration, driven in part by the inability of Christian institutions to thrive under these laws, threatens to further reduce the already dwindling Christian population in the Holy Land.

Despite these challenges, Christian leaders and organizations continue to advocate for their right to build and maintain their institutions. Churches have launched legal battles, appealing to both Israeli courts and international bodies to challenge the discriminatory zoning laws that are suffocating their communities. While some small victories have been achieved, the overall environment remains hostile, with the Israeli government showing little willingness to ease its restrictions on Palestinian Christian construction.

The discriminatory zoning and building laws imposed by Israel are not just about limiting physical development—they are a tool of political control, designed to suppress the growth and influence of

Palestinian Christian communities. By restricting the expansion and restoration of churches and community buildings, these laws are slowly eroding the ability of Christian institutions to serve their people. The result is a community under siege, forced into decline by policies that favor settlers and undermine the rich religious and cultural heritage of Christianity in the Holy Land.

Citizenship and Residency Struggles: The Fight to Stay in Jerusalem

FOR PALESTINIAN CHRISTIANS, especially those living in Jerusalem, retaining residency rights has become a daunting challenge. Under Israeli law, Palestinian residents of East Jerusalem, including Christians, face a complex and often discriminatory legal system that puts their residency status at constant risk. One of the most significant challenges is the "center of life" policy, which effectively revokes residency rights for Palestinians who live or spend extended time outside the city. This policy has caused immense hardship for Palestinian Christians, many of whom have family, work, or education-related reasons to spend time outside Jerusalem. The result is a legal framework that erodes their right to remain in the city, forcing many into a precarious and uncertain existence.

Since Israel's annexation of East Jerusalem in 1967, Palestinian residents have not been granted full Israeli citizenship. Instead, they are categorized as "permanent residents," a status that is far more vulnerable to revocation than citizenship. This residency status comes with a number of limitations, including restrictions on travel, voting, and access to services. However, the most troubling aspect is the ease with which residency can be revoked under Israeli law. For Palestinian Christians, losing residency rights means losing the ability to live in Jerusalem—the city that holds profound religious and cultural significance for them.

The "center of life" policy is one of the main tools used by Israeli authorities to strip Palestinians of their residency rights. According to this policy, residents of East Jerusalem must prove that Jerusalem is their primary place of residence and that their "center of life" is within the city's municipal boundaries. This means that they must provide documentation showing that they live, work, and send their children to school in Jerusalem. For Palestinian Christians, this can be especially difficult. Many have family members living in other parts of the West Bank, or they may need to spend extended periods outside the city for work or education. Even something as simple as temporarily moving to a nearby town or traveling abroad for an extended period can result in residency revocation.

The consequences of losing residency status are severe. Once residency is revoked, Palestinians lose the right to live in Jerusalem, and they are barred from returning to the city without special permits, which are difficult to obtain. This often leads to family separation, as individuals who lose their residency are forced to move to the West Bank or other areas, leaving behind their homes, communities, and churches in Jerusalem. For many Christian families, the threat of losing their residency status has created a constant sense of insecurity, as they must carefully navigate the legal system and avoid any action that could be interpreted as a shift in their "center of life."

In addition to the "center of life" policy, other legal barriers make it difficult for Palestinian Christians to retain their residency in Jerusalem. For example, when a Palestinian resident of Jerusalem marries someone from the West Bank or Gaza, their spouse is not automatically granted residency in the city. Instead, they must go through a long and complicated process to apply for family unification, which is often denied or delayed for years. This legal hurdle has forced many Christian couples to live separately, with one spouse residing in Jerusalem and the other in the West Bank, further fracturing the social fabric of Christian communities in the city.

The restrictions on residency are compounded by the broader political environment in Jerusalem. Israeli authorities have actively pursued policies that seek to reduce the Palestinian population in the city while encouraging Jewish settlement. These policies include the expansion of Jewish neighborhoods in East Jerusalem and the demolition of Palestinian homes deemed to have been built without proper permits—a problem exacerbated by the difficulty Palestinians face in obtaining building permits in the first place. This political strategy has made it clear that the Israeli government views the presence of Palestinians in Jerusalem, including Christians, as an obstacle to its long-term vision for the city.

For Palestinian Christians, the struggle to maintain residency in Jerusalem is not just a legal battle—it is a fight to preserve their cultural and religious identity in one of the most important cities in the Christian world. Jerusalem is home to many of Christianity's most sacred sites, including the Church of the Holy Sepulchre, and has been a center of Christian life for centuries. Losing the right to live in the city means losing access to these holy places and being disconnected from the heart of their faith. It also means the gradual erosion of the Christian community in Jerusalem, as more and more families are forced to leave, reducing the Christian population to a small, marginalized minority.

The process of proving residency status is both invasive and bureaucratically complex. Palestinian Christians must regularly provide documentation to Israeli authorities to prove that their "center of life" remains in Jerusalem. This includes submitting utility bills, tax receipts, school enrollment records, and other forms of evidence. Failure to provide sufficient documentation can result in the loss of residency status. For many families, this process is not only stressful but also financially burdensome, as they are forced to navigate a legal system designed to work against them.

Despite these challenges, Palestinian Christians continue to resist the efforts to revoke their residency and maintain their presence in Jerusalem. Churches and Christian organizations have been active in advocating for the rights of their communities, providing legal assistance and social support to those at risk of losing their residency. However, the broader political and legal environment remains hostile, with little indication that Israeli authorities are willing to ease the restrictions on Palestinian residency rights.

The struggle for residency in Jerusalem is a reflection of the broader challenges faced by Palestinian Christians living under occupation. As Israeli laws and policies continue to target their rights and presence in the city, the future of the Christian community in Jerusalem becomes increasingly precarious. Without significant legal and political changes, the gradual displacement of Palestinian Christians from Jerusalem will continue, further diminishing the Christian presence in the city that holds such deep religious and historical importance.

Chapter 4: The Struggle of Palestinian Christian Churches: A Fight for Survival

The churches of Palestine, once central to the spiritual and communal life of local Christians, now find themselves caught in a struggle for survival. Under Israeli occupation, these churches face a host of challenges that threaten their very existence. From legal battles to retain ownership of holy sites, to the financial hardships brought on by economic instability and shrinking congregations, Palestinian Christian churches are under immense pressure. Israeli policies have not only restricted their ability to function and grow but have also isolated them from the global Christian community, leaving these institutions in a precarious position. For Palestinian Christians, the churches represent more than just places of worship; they are cultural and historical anchors that connect them to their faith and to each other. Yet, under occupation, their future remains uncertain.

The legal battle to preserve holy sites is one of the most pressing issues facing Palestinian Christian churches. Many of these churches hold historic significance, marking key moments in Christian history, such as the Church of the Nativity in Bethlehem and the Church of the Holy Sepulchre in Jerusalem. These sites not only attract pilgrims from around the world but also serve as symbols of the enduring Christian presence in the Holy Land. However, Israeli authorities and Jewish settler organizations have increasingly targeted church-owned properties, seeking to seize land through legal loopholes, absentee property laws, and questionable real estate deals. Christian churches have been forced to fight lengthy and expensive legal battles to retain ownership of these holy sites, often with limited success. The constant threat of land confiscation hangs over many churches, as they struggle to protect the properties that have been in their care for centuries.

The fight to preserve these holy sites is not just about property rights; it is about maintaining the religious and cultural identity of Palestinian Christians. As these churches face legal challenges, the broader Christian community in Palestine becomes more vulnerable. The loss of church land not only diminishes the ability of the church to serve its congregation but also weakens the Christian presence in a region where they are already a minority. The ongoing legal struggles, combined with the physical encroachment of Israeli settlements, have left many churches in a state of uncertainty, unsure of how long they will be able to hold onto their historic properties.

Financial hardships have further compounded the difficulties faced by Palestinian Christian churches. The economic instability brought on by the Israeli occupation, coupled with the restrictions on movement and access to resources, has left many churches struggling to stay afloat. In the past, churches could rely on income from pilgrimage tourism and local donations to support their activities. However, the construction of the Separation Wall and the imposition of military checkpoints have severely restricted the flow of pilgrims to key Christian sites, cutting off a vital source of revenue. As a result, many churches are facing severe financial shortfalls, which limit their ability to maintain their buildings, support their clergy, and provide essential services to their congregations.

The shrinking Christian population in Palestine has also contributed to the financial strain on churches. As more Palestinian Christians emigrate in search of better opportunities, church attendance has declined, leaving many parishes with smaller and less financially stable congregations. This decline in membership makes it increasingly difficult for churches to raise the funds needed to keep their doors open and to continue their religious and social missions.

The emigration of Christians, driven by economic hardship and political instability, has created a vicious cycle, as shrinking congregations lead to weakened churches, which in turn accelerates the departure of more Christians.

Isolation, both local and global, has further exacerbated the struggles of Palestinian Christian churches. Israeli policies have severely restricted the ability of these churches to connect with the global Christian community, cutting them off from the financial, political, and moral support they once received. International Christian organizations and churches, which have historically provided aid and assistance to Palestinian Christians, often face bureaucratic obstacles when trying to deliver help. Israeli authorities frequently delay or deny the issuance of permits required for international clergy, aid workers, and supplies to reach Palestinian churches, leaving them increasingly isolated from the broader Christian world.

This isolation is not only economic but also political. Palestinian Christian churches are often caught in the middle of the broader Israeli-Palestinian conflict, with little political leverage to advocate for their own interests. While they share many of the same challenges as their Muslim neighbors, Christian churches are often overlooked in international diplomacy and media coverage, further isolating them from potential sources of support. The lack of international attention to their plight has left Palestinian Christian churches feeling abandoned, both by their own governments and by the global Christian community.

Despite these immense challenges, Palestinian Christian churches continue to play a vital role in the lives of their congregants. They provide not only spiritual guidance but also essential social services, such as education, healthcare, and charity, to both Christians and Muslims in their communities. However, without significant changes to the legal, economic, and political environment in which they operate, these churches face an uncertain future. The ongoing struggle to preserve their holy sites, maintain financial stability, and overcome local and global isolation is a testament to the resilience of Palestinian Christians, but it is a struggle that they cannot sustain indefinitely without greater support.

The struggle of Palestinian Christian churches is emblematic of the broader challenges faced by the entire Christian community in Palestine. These institutions, which have stood as pillars of faith and culture for centuries, are now fighting for survival in a land that has become increasingly hostile to their presence. As the legal battles over land ownership continue, as financial hardships grow, and as international support remains limited, the future of these churches—and of Christianity in the Holy Land itself—hangs in the balance.

The Fight to Preserve Holy Sites: Defending Christian Heritage Against Seizure

FOR CENTURIES, THE Christian holy sites in Palestine have been pillars of faith, culture, and history, standing as testaments to the enduring presence of Christianity in the Holy Land. These sites—such as the Church of the Nativity in Bethlehem and the Church of the Holy Sepulchre in Jerusalem—are not only places of deep religious significance but also symbols of Christian heritage and identity. However, in recent years, the churches that oversee these sacred spaces have faced escalating legal battles to retain ownership of their historic properties. As Israeli authorities and Jewish settler organizations increasingly target these sites for seizure, the fight to preserve Christian holy sites has become a critical struggle for the survival of Christian communities in Palestine.

One of the most significant challenges facing Christian churches in Palestine is the application of Israeli laws that allow the state to confiscate properties under various legal pretexts. The Absentee

Property Law is one of the most frequently used tools by the Israeli government to claim ownership of church-owned lands. Enacted in 1950, this law permits the Israeli government to seize land from Palestinians—including Christians—who were displaced during the 1948 war or who are deemed "absent" from their properties. This has led to the confiscation of numerous Christian-owned properties, particularly in East Jerusalem, where church lands are often targeted for settlement expansion. Despite the historical and religious significance of these properties, Israeli authorities have applied the law indiscriminately, stripping churches of their rightful ownership.

The Church of the Nativity in Bethlehem, one of Christianity's most revered sites, has been at the center of legal struggles over property rights. While the church itself remains under Christian control, the land surrounding it has been the subject of numerous disputes as Israeli settlers seek to expand their presence in the area. Christian leaders have had to engage in protracted legal battles to prevent encroachment on these lands, often facing overwhelming odds in an Israeli court system that tends to favor settlers. These legal battles drain church resources, as the cost of defending their properties in court mounts over time, making it even harder for the churches to focus on their primary mission of serving their communities.

The Church of the Holy Sepulchre in Jerusalem, considered by many to be the holiest site in Christianity, has also faced threats to its surrounding properties. In recent years, Israeli settler organizations have made aggressive efforts to purchase or claim ownership of properties near the church, hoping to establish a stronger Jewish presence in the Old City. The Greek Orthodox Church, which holds significant properties in the area, has been locked in legal disputes with these groups, attempting to block the sale or transfer of land that has been in Christian hands for centuries. However, these legal battles are often complicated by political pressures and the involvement of powerful settler organizations backed by government support.

In addition to these direct threats, Christian churches face the ongoing challenge of maintaining their properties under the weight of restrictive Israeli building and zoning laws. Churches seeking to renovate or restore their buildings, many of which are hundreds of years old, often encounter bureaucratic obstacles that delay or prevent necessary repairs. This is particularly troubling for churches that rely on their properties not only for religious purposes but also for economic activities, such as pilgrim accommodations or agriculture, which help fund their operations. Without the ability to maintain and protect these properties, Christian institutions are left vulnerable to further erosion of their land and influence.

Another layer of complexity in these legal battles is the involvement of international actors, who at times have sought to mediate or provide support to the churches in their fight to retain their holy sites. The Vatican, for example, has been an advocate for the preservation of Christian sites in the Holy Land, often intervening diplomatically to protect these properties from seizure. However, international intervention has its limits, as the Israeli government retains ultimate control over land disputes within its jurisdiction. Diplomatic pressure can only go so far when faced with a legal system that prioritizes the interests of settlers over the historical and religious rights of Christian institutions.

The legal battles over Christian holy sites are not just about property; they are about the preservation of a cultural and spiritual heritage that is deeply intertwined with the identity of Palestinian Christians. These sites represent more than just land—they are sacred spaces that have been passed down through generations, places where Christians have worshipped, celebrated, and mourned for centuries. The threat of losing these holy sites to Israeli seizure is a direct attack on the continuity of Christian life in the Holy Land, as the loss of these properties would further diminish the already shrinking Christian presence in the region.

The ongoing struggle to protect and maintain these sites is a reflection of the broader challenges faced by Palestinian Christians, who are increasingly marginalized by both the Israeli occupation and the political realities of the conflict. As the Israeli government continues to support settlement expansion and the confiscation of Palestinian land, Christian churches find themselves on the front lines of a battle to preserve their faith's most sacred places. The legal, financial, and political pressures they face are immense, and without significant changes in policy, the future of these sites—and the Christian communities that rely on them—remains uncertain.

Despite the difficulties, Christian churches continue to fight to preserve their holy sites. They engage in legal battles, mobilize international support, and resist encroachment from settlers, determined to protect the places that hold such deep meaning for their faith and history. However, the stakes are high, and the future of Christianity in the Holy Land is increasingly tied to the outcome of these legal struggles. As churches continue to face threats to their properties, their fight to preserve holy sites is not just a legal matter—it is a battle for the survival of Christian heritage in the land where it all began.

Financial Hardships and Shrinking Congregations: The Economic Decline of Palestinian Christian Churches

THE CHURCHES IN PALESTINE have long been central to the lives of local Christian communities, providing spiritual guidance, education, healthcare, and social services. However, the economic challenges brought on by Israeli occupation, restrictions on movement, and the steady emigration of Christians have severely weakened the financial stability of these institutions. Palestinian Christian churches now find themselves grappling with dwindling resources, shrinking congregations, and the mounting difficulties of operating in a context where their ability to generate income and sustain their activities is increasingly compromised. The economic decline of local churches not only affects their religious mission but also threatens the survival of Christian communities in the Holy Land.

One of the most significant factors contributing to the financial struggles of Palestinian Christian churches is the severe economic hardship imposed by the Israeli occupation. Churches in Bethlehem, Jerusalem, and other parts of the West Bank once relied heavily on income generated from tourism, particularly Christian pilgrimage. Pilgrims visiting sites like the Church of the Nativity and the Church of the Holy Sepulchre would bring vital financial support to local churches, either through donations or by using church-owned guesthouses, shops, and services. However, the construction of the Separation Wall, combined with military checkpoints and restrictions on movement, has drastically reduced the flow of pilgrims to these sites. Many would-be visitors are deterred by the difficulties of navigating the West Bank, and those who do come often find themselves limited in their ability to access Christian communities that are cut off by the Wall and other barriers.

The economic impact of this decline in pilgrimage tourism has been devastating for Palestinian Christian churches. Without the steady flow of visitors, churches have lost a major source of revenue that they relied on to fund their operations. This loss of income has affected the ability of churches to maintain their buildings, pay clergy and staff, and continue providing essential services to their congregations. The financial strain is particularly acute for churches that own large properties, such as monasteries and guesthouses, which require significant upkeep but no longer generate the necessary revenue to remain operational. As a result, many churches are now struggling to make ends meet, with some forced to reduce their activities or close parts of their operations altogether.

Another major challenge facing Palestinian Christian churches is the shrinking size of their congregations. The ongoing political instability, economic hardship, and lack of opportunities have led many Palestinian Christians to emigrate in search of better lives abroad. Over the past several decades, the Christian population in Palestine has steadily declined, with thousands leaving for countries in Europe, North America, and Latin America. This exodus has left many churches with much smaller congregations, reducing the amount of local donations that once supported church activities. The loss of parishioners not only affects the financial viability of the churches but also weakens the social fabric of Christian communities, as families are split apart and long-standing connections are severed.

In addition to the financial impact of emigration, restrictions on movement within the West Bank have made it difficult for even those who remain to attend church regularly. Israeli checkpoints, roadblocks, and the Separation Wall create significant obstacles for Palestinian Christians who wish to travel to their churches, especially those located in different towns or cities. This has further reduced church attendance, as many congregants find it too difficult or dangerous to make the journey to worship. For churches in smaller, more isolated communities, these restrictions have been particularly damaging, as the already limited number of parishioners continues to dwindle.

The financial hardships facing Palestinian Christian churches have also affected their ability to provide social services to their communities. Many churches run schools, hospitals, and charitable organizations that serve both Christians and Muslims in the West Bank. However, as their financial resources have dried up, these institutions have struggled to continue their work. Christian schools, which once provided education to thousands of Palestinian children, are finding it harder to cover their operating costs, leading to staff cuts, reduced services, and in some cases, closures. Hospitals and clinics, which have long been lifelines for local communities, are similarly under strain, as the churches that support them can no longer afford to subsidize their operations.

The isolation of Palestinian Christian churches from the global Christian community has further exacerbated their financial struggles. In the past, churches in Palestine often received significant support from international Christian organizations, particularly those based in Europe and North America. However, Israeli policies have made it increasingly difficult for international aid to reach Palestinian churches. Bureaucratic obstacles, such as restrictions on foreign clergy, limitations on the transfer of funds, and delays in the delivery of supplies, have cut off many churches from the financial and logistical assistance they once relied on. This isolation has left Palestinian Christian churches increasingly vulnerable, as they struggle to sustain themselves without the support of the wider Christian world.

The financial hardships facing Palestinian Christian churches are not just an economic problem; they are a threat to the survival of Christianity in the Holy Land. As churches lose the resources needed to maintain their buildings, pay their clergy, and serve their communities, the Christian presence in Palestine continues to shrink. For many Palestinian Christians, the church is not only a place of worship but also a vital part of their social and cultural identity. The decline of these institutions risks further eroding the Christian community, as more families emigrate or become disconnected from their faith.

Despite these challenges, Palestinian Christian churches continue to fight for their survival. Church leaders are actively seeking ways to adapt to the new economic realities, exploring alternative sources of income and appealing for international support. However, without significant changes to the political and economic conditions in which they operate, these churches face an uncertain future. The financial hardships and shrinking congregations that have weakened Palestinian Christian churches are part of a broader pattern of decline that threatens the very existence of Christianity in the land where it was born.

Local and Global Isolation: The Restriction of Palestinian Christian Churches

ISRAELI POLICIES HAVE not only affected the day-to-day lives of Palestinian Christians but have also systematically isolated their churches, cutting them off from the global Christian community. This isolation is both political and economic, as Palestinian Christian churches struggle to maintain connections with international organizations, clergy, and aid networks that once provided essential support. Over time, these restrictions have weakened the churches' ability to function effectively, exacerbating their financial difficulties and undermining their influence on the global stage.

One of the key ways in which Israeli policies have isolated Palestinian Christian churches is through restrictions on travel and access. The Separation Wall, military checkpoints, and strict permit requirements make it extremely difficult for Palestinian Christians to travel between cities within the West Bank, let alone travel internationally. Christian clergy and church leaders who need to visit churches in other parts of the region or abroad must navigate a complex and often opaque permit system. Many are denied permits altogether, leaving churches disconnected from the broader Christian world. Even within Palestine, church leaders face severe limitations when trying to reach congregants in different cities, as the Israeli military controls key routes between Christian towns like Bethlehem, Jerusalem, and Nazareth.

This internal isolation has had a profound impact on the spiritual and communal life of Palestinian Christian churches. Without the ability to freely interact with one another, churches are left fragmented, unable to coordinate on important religious, social, or political matters. Churches that once worked together to host regional events, celebrate religious festivals, or support local initiatives now struggle to maintain even basic communication. This lack of connection weakens the Christian community as a whole, as churches are forced to operate in isolation, without the strength that comes from unity and cooperation.

Beyond internal restrictions, Israeli policies have also made it increasingly difficult for Palestinian Christian churches to connect with the global Christian community. In the past, churches in Palestine had strong ties with Christian organizations and churches in Europe, North America, and other parts of the world. These international relationships provided not only spiritual solidarity but also vital financial and logistical support. Many churches relied on donations from abroad to fund their operations, maintain their buildings, and support social services like schools and hospitals. However, Israeli policies have systematically undermined these connections, isolating Palestinian churches from the outside world.

One of the main tools of this isolation is the restriction of foreign clergy and aid workers. In many cases, international clergy who wish to serve in Palestinian churches are denied visas or face significant delays in obtaining the necessary permits to enter Israel and the West Bank. This has left many Palestinian churches understaffed, as local clergy are stretched thin trying to cover multiple parishes with fewer resources. The absence of international clergy also deprives Palestinian churches of a crucial link to the global Christian community, as these foreign clergy often serve as bridges between local churches and their counterparts abroad.

Similarly, international Christian organizations that wish to provide financial or humanitarian aid to Palestinian churches face bureaucratic hurdles that make it nearly impossible to deliver assistance. Israeli authorities often delay or deny the importation of supplies, including food, medicine, and building materials, that are meant to support church-run schools, hospitals, and charities. Financial transfers from international donors are also subject to intense scrutiny, with Israeli regulations making it difficult for churches to access the funds they need to continue their work. These obstacles have left Palestinian Christian churches increasingly dependent on dwindling local resources, even as their financial needs grow.

The political isolation of Palestinian Christian churches is perhaps most evident in their diminishing visibility on the international stage. As Israeli policies continue to restrict access and communication, the plight of Palestinian Christians receives less attention from the global Christian community. Many international Christian organizations, particularly those in Europe and North America, are unaware of the full extent of the challenges faced by Palestinian churches, in part because the Israeli government controls the narrative and limits access to these communities. This lack of visibility means that Palestinian churches are often overlooked in global discussions about religious freedom, human rights, and the Israeli-Palestinian conflict.

At the same time, Israeli authorities have worked to strengthen relationships with certain Christian groups abroad, particularly those that align with the political goals of the Israeli state. This has further marginalized Palestinian Christian churches, which are often seen as politically inconvenient due to their opposition to the occupation and their support for Palestinian rights. By promoting ties with international Christian Zionist organizations, which support Israeli policies, the Israeli government has deepened the isolation of Palestinian Christian churches from the broader Christian world. This selective engagement with Christian groups has created divisions within global Christianity, as many Christians abroad remain unaware of the struggles faced by their Palestinian counterparts.

The economic consequences of this isolation are severe. Without access to international support, Palestinian Christian churches struggle to maintain their financial stability. The loss of international donations, coupled with the challenges of sustaining local congregations in an economically depressed environment, has left many churches on the brink of financial collapse. Churches that once relied on pilgrimage tourism and foreign aid to support their activities are now forced to operate with minimal resources, cutting back on services and struggling to maintain their buildings. The financial isolation of Palestinian churches threatens their long-term viability, as they are increasingly unable to fulfill their religious and social missions.

Despite these challenges, Palestinian Christian churches continue to resist the isolation imposed on them. They seek to maintain their connections with the global Christian community, even in the face of bureaucratic and political obstacles. Church leaders engage in advocacy, both locally and internationally, to raise awareness about their plight and to call for greater support from the global Christian world. However, the structural barriers created by Israeli policies make it increasingly difficult for these churches to break free from the isolation that threatens their future.

The isolation of Palestinian Christian churches is not just a local issue; it is a global one. The ability of these churches to survive and thrive depends in large part on their ability to connect with the broader Christian community, both spiritually and financially. As long as Israeli policies continue to restrict their movement, access, and communication, Palestinian Christian churches will remain isolated, struggling to preserve their presence in the Holy Land. Without greater international attention and support, the churches that have stood for centuries as beacons of Christian faith in Palestine may be left to fade into obscurity, disconnected from the world and from their own history.

Chapter 5: Economic Dispossession: How Jewish Settlements Destroy Christian Livelihoods

The expansion of Jewish settlements across the West Bank and East Jerusalem has profoundly impacted the Palestinian Christian community, stripping many of their livelihoods and undermining the economic foundations that have sustained them for generations. While much of the focus on settlements highlights their impact on the broader Palestinian population, the consequences for Christians have been particularly severe. These settlements have displaced Christian families, taken over farmland, and deprived Christian farmers and business owners of their traditional sources of income. Backed by extensive Israeli government support, the growth of settlements has not only eroded the land but has also pushed Palestinian Christians to the margins of society, leaving them economically vulnerable and with few options for survival.

One of the most destructive impacts of settlement expansion has been the displacement of Christian families from their homes and lands. As Israeli settlements grow, they encroach on areas that have been home to Palestinian Christians for centuries. In places like Bethlehem and Beit Jala, Christian families have found themselves hemmed in by settlements, with their land either confiscated by the Israeli government or rendered inaccessible due to the construction of security barriers and roads reserved for settlers. Entire Christian communities have been displaced, with families forced to leave behind their homes, churches, and schools in search of safety and stability elsewhere. The result is the gradual fragmentation of Christian society, as families are scattered and communities are broken apart.

The expansion of settlements has also led to the seizure of Christian-owned farmland, which has historically been a critical source of income for many families. For generations, Palestinian Christians have relied on agriculture—particularly olive farming—as a means of supporting their families and communities. However, as settlements spread, large swaths of agricultural land have been confiscated or cut off from their owners. Settlers, often with the backing of the Israeli military, have taken over these lands, uprooting olive trees and building homes, farms, and outposts. Christian farmers are left with little recourse, as legal challenges to reclaim their land are either ignored or stalled indefinitely in Israeli courts.

The loss of agricultural land has been devastating for Christian farmers, who have seen their primary source of livelihood disappear. In some cases, entire orchards have been destroyed to make way for settlement expansion, leaving farmers with nothing to harvest or sell. This economic dispossession has forced many Christian families to abandon their traditional way of life and seek other forms of employment, often in low-paying jobs that do not provide the same stability or income. For those who remain in farming, the challenges of accessing their land—due to military checkpoints, settler violence, and restricted movement—make it nearly impossible to sustain their agricultural operations. The result is an economic downward spiral, as Christian farmers are gradually driven out of their lands and forced into poverty.

The role of the Israeli government in supporting settlements has further marginalized Palestinian Christian communities. The government provides extensive subsidies, infrastructure, and security for settlers, creating a stark contrast between the well-supported settlements and the neglected Palestinian communities nearby. Settlers benefit from government-funded roads, water supplies, electricity, and security forces, all of which make their presence in the West Bank not only sustainable but also economically attractive. Meanwhile, Palestinian Christians living nearby receive little to no government support, and they often face discriminatory policies that restrict their access to basic services.

This disparity in support has allowed settlements to flourish while Christian communities are left to wither. Israeli settlers, who receive financial incentives to move to the West Bank, are able to build homes, establish businesses, and live relatively prosperous lives, even as their Palestinian Christian neighbors struggle to make ends meet. The government's support for settlements has created an uneven playing field, where Palestinian Christians are economically disadvantaged and systematically excluded from the benefits of growth and development. This economic marginalization has forced many Christian families to emigrate, leaving behind the lands and livelihoods they have held for generations.

One particularly egregious example of this dispossession is the Cremisan Valley, where Christian farmers have been engaged in a long legal battle to protect their land from Israeli settlement expansion and the construction of the Separation Wall. The valley, home to the Cremisan Monastery and its vineyards, has historically provided income and sustenance for Christian families in the area. However, Israeli authorities have sought to build the Wall through the valley, effectively cutting off farmers from their land and jeopardizing their livelihoods. Despite international outcry and support from the Vatican, much of the land has been confiscated, and the farmers' ability to work their fields has been severely restricted. The case of Cremisan illustrates the broader pattern of land confiscation that has devastated Palestinian Christian farmers and left them with few options for economic survival.

The loss of agricultural land and the displacement of Christian communities are part of a broader strategy of economic dispossession that has targeted Palestinian Christians, along with their Muslim neighbors. The settlements, supported by the Israeli government, have systematically undermined the economic foundations of Christian life in Palestine, pushing families into poverty and forcing them to abandon their homes and land. As Christian communities shrink and their economic base erodes, the future of Palestinian Christianity in the Holy Land becomes increasingly uncertain.

The economic dispossession caused by settlement expansion is not just a local issue; it has far-reaching implications for the Christian presence in the Holy Land. As more and more Christian families are forced to leave due to economic hardship, the Christian population in Palestine continues to decline. This threatens the survival of a community that has been an integral part of the region's history for two millennia. Without land, income, or government support, Palestinian Christians find themselves on the margins of society, struggling to hold onto their identity and heritage in a land that has become increasingly hostile to their presence.

The Expansion of Settlements: Displacing Christian Families and Destroying Livelihoods

THE EXPANSION OF JEWISH settlements in the West Bank and East Jerusalem has had a profound and devastating impact on Palestinian Christian communities. For decades, the steady growth of these settlements has systematically displaced Christian families, confiscated farmland, and destroyed the traditional sources of income that have sustained these communities for generations. Backed by Israeli government policies and military enforcement, the expansion of settlements has not only altered the physical landscape but also eroded the social and economic foundations of Christian life in Palestine, leaving many families struggling to survive.

One of the most immediate and visible effects of settlement expansion has been the displacement of Christian families from their homes and communities. As settlements spread, they encroach on Palestinian-owned land, often with little to no warning. Christian families, many of whom have lived on their land for generations, find themselves forced to leave as their homes are confiscated or demolished to make way for new settlement construction. In areas like Beit Jala and Bethlehem, where Christian populations have historically been concentrated, the growth of nearby settlements has left many families with no choice but to relocate, severing their ties to their land, churches, and communities.

This displacement is often accompanied by the confiscation of farmland, which has long been a critical source of income for Palestinian Christian families. Farming, particularly olive cultivation, has been a traditional way of life for many Christians in the West Bank. However, as settlements expand, large portions of farmland are seized or rendered inaccessible due to military-enforced security zones, roads, and fences. Olive groves, vineyards, and other agricultural lands that have sustained Christian families for generations are either taken over by settlers or destroyed to clear the way for new settlement infrastructure. This loss of farmland is not only a blow to the economic stability of Christian families but also a symbolic loss, as the land is deeply tied to their cultural and historical identity.

In many cases, settlers directly target Christian farmland, uprooting olive trees and destroying crops to assert their control over the land. These actions are often carried out with the tacit approval of Israeli authorities, who provide security for the settlers and fail to intervene when Palestinian land is seized or damaged. The destruction of farmland has left many Christian families without their primary source of income, forcing them to seek low-paying jobs in other sectors or rely on aid from churches and international organizations. The economic consequences of settlement expansion are particularly severe for families who have traditionally relied on agriculture to support themselves, as the loss of land means the loss of their livelihoods.

The expansion of settlements has also deprived Palestinian Christians of access to essential resources such as water and infrastructure. Many settlements are built on land that was once used by Palestinian farmers, and they often tap into water resources that were previously available to local communities. As a result, Palestinian Christians face water shortages and struggle to irrigate their remaining farmland, further diminishing their ability to grow crops and sustain their livelihoods. Meanwhile, settlers benefit from state-of-the-art infrastructure, including roads, electricity, and water systems, all of which are heavily subsidized by the Israeli government. This unequal distribution of resources exacerbates the economic hardships faced by Palestinian Christians, who are left with few opportunities for growth or development.

The construction of Israeli-only roads and infrastructure that connect settlements to major cities like Jerusalem has also contributed to the isolation and economic marginalization of Palestinian Christians. These roads often cut through Palestinian land, dividing communities and making it difficult for farmers and business owners to access their fields or transport goods to market. The presence of military checkpoints and barriers along these roads further restricts movement, creating a climate of fear and uncertainty for Palestinian Christians who are trying to maintain their livelihoods under increasingly oppressive conditions.

The impact of settlement expansion on Christian families is not limited to economic loss; it also has profound social and psychological effects. The displacement of families from their homes and land has fractured Christian communities, breaking apart long-standing social networks and support systems. As more Christian families are forced to emigrate in search of economic stability and safety, the Christian population in Palestine continues to shrink, leaving behind smaller and more vulnerable communities. This demographic shift has weakened the overall presence of Christians in the Holy Land, making it more difficult for the remaining families to sustain their religious and cultural traditions.

Despite these challenges, Palestinian Christian communities continue to resist the pressures of settlement expansion. Churches and local organizations have mobilized to provide support for displaced families, offering legal aid, financial assistance, and social services to those affected by land confiscation and economic hardship. However, the scale of settlement expansion and the lack of meaningful intervention from the Israeli government or international actors make it increasingly difficult for these efforts to have a lasting impact.

The expansion of Jewish settlements has been a central factor in the economic and social decline of Palestinian Christian communities. By displacing families, seizing farmland, and depriving Christians of their traditional sources of income, settlement expansion has fundamentally altered the landscape of Christian life in Palestine. The loss of land and livelihoods, combined with the ongoing pressure of emigration, threatens the long-term survival of Christian communities in the Holy Land. As settlements continue to grow, the future of Palestinian Christians becomes increasingly uncertain, as they struggle to hold onto their land, their homes, and their identity in the face of relentless dispossession.

The Role of Israeli Government Support for Settlers: Marginalizing Palestinian Christian Communities

THE EXPANSION OF JEWISH settlements in the West Bank and East Jerusalem has been heavily supported by the Israeli government through a combination of subsidies, infrastructure development, and legal protections. This government backing has played a key role in the rapid growth of settlements, offering settlers economic incentives and state-of-the-art infrastructure that enable them to thrive, while simultaneously deepening the economic marginalization of Palestinian Christian communities. By prioritizing the needs of settlers over those of Palestinians, including Christians, the Israeli government has created an environment in which the economic disparities between settlers and Palestinian Christians continue to widen, leaving the latter increasingly vulnerable and marginalized.

One of the most significant ways the Israeli government supports settlers is through direct financial subsidies. These subsidies take various forms, including tax breaks, grants for housing construction, and incentives for businesses to relocate to the settlements. Settlers are often given access to affordable housing and land, making it financially attractive for Israelis to move to the West Bank. In contrast, Palestinian Christian families, who have lived on their land for generations, are frequently denied permits to build new homes or expand their properties, forcing them to live in overcrowded conditions or move elsewhere. This disparity in housing opportunities has contributed to the economic strain on Palestinian Christian communities, who are unable to compete with the government-backed growth of settlements.

In addition to housing subsidies, the Israeli government invests heavily in infrastructure development for settlements. Roads, water systems, electricity, and other essential services are provided at a high standard to support the settlers' quality of life. Roads that connect settlements to major cities like Jerusalem and Tel Aviv are often built on confiscated Palestinian land, further displacing local communities. These roads, which are typically reserved for the exclusive use of settlers, not only fragment Palestinian territory but also restrict the movement of Palestinian Christians, who must navigate military checkpoints and security barriers just to reach their farms, schools, or workplaces. The restricted access to infrastructure limits Palestinian

Christians' ability to sustain their livelihoods, as they are cut off from markets and economic opportunities.

Water allocation is another area where Israeli government support for settlers directly impacts Palestinian Christian communities. Settlements often receive a disproportionate share of water resources, allowing settlers to irrigate their crops, fill swimming pools, and maintain green spaces. Meanwhile, Palestinian Christians living nearby face severe water shortages, struggling to irrigate their farmland or even meet basic household needs. The unequal distribution of water has had devastating consequences for Christian farmers, many of whom have been forced to abandon their land because they can no longer cultivate crops or sustain livestock. This loss of agricultural productivity further impoverishes Christian families, who have traditionally relied on farming as their primary source of income.

The Israeli government's support for settlers extends beyond financial subsidies and infrastructure; it also includes legal protections and military enforcement. Settlers who encroach on Palestinian land, including land owned by Christian churches and families, are often shielded from legal consequences. When Palestinian Christians attempt to challenge land confiscation in Israeli courts, they face lengthy legal battles with little chance of success, as the legal system is heavily biased in favor of settlers. Even in cases where courts rule in favor of Palestinians, enforcement of these rulings is rare, and settlers often remain on the land with the protection of the Israeli military. This legal impunity allows settlers to continue expanding their presence on Palestinian land, further eroding the economic base of Christian communities.

The Israeli military plays a key role in enforcing policies that favor settlers and marginalize Palestinian Christians. Military checkpoints, security barriers, and restricted access zones are all designed to protect settlers and ensure their free movement, while Palestinian Christians are subjected to constant surveillance and restrictions on their mobility. These measures create significant barriers to economic activity, as Christian farmers, business owners, and workers are unable to travel freely to their fields, markets, or workplaces. The presence of settlers and the military infrastructure that supports them has turned many areas of the West Bank into isolated enclaves, where Palestinian Christians struggle to maintain their livelihoods under the constant threat of displacement and violence.

The cumulative effect of Israeli government support for settlers is the systematic economic marginalization of Palestinian Christian communities. As settlers receive state-backed advantages in housing, infrastructure, and legal protections, Palestinian Christians are left to contend with a hostile environment in which their economic prospects are severely limited. The loss of land, restricted access to resources, and legal discrimination have forced many Christian families to emigrate, seeking better opportunities abroad. This steady exodus has further weakened the Christian presence in the Holy Land, as shrinking congregations and communities struggle to sustain their cultural and religious heritage.

While settlers benefit from the full support of the Israeli government, Palestinian Christians are excluded from these opportunities and resources. The government's prioritization of settlement expansion over the rights of indigenous Palestinian communities has created a deeply unequal system, where Christian families are pushed to the margins and deprived of their economic independence. As the settlements continue to grow, bolstered by state support, the future of Palestinian Christian communities becomes increasingly uncertain, as they face not only the loss of their land but also the erosion of their livelihoods and cultural identity.

The Loss of Agricultural Land: Christian Farmers Left with Little Economic Recourse

FOR GENERATIONS, PALESTINIAN Christian farmers have relied on their agricultural lands to support their families and sustain their communities. Olive groves, vineyards, and other crops have been central to the economic and cultural life of these communities, forming an essential part of their identity and livelihoods. However, the expansion of Israeli settlements has systematically eroded access to these lands, displacing Christian farmers and leaving them with few options for survival. As settlements grow, more and more agricultural land is confiscated or made inaccessible, depriving Christian farmers of their traditional source of income and pushing them into economic despair.

One notable example of this loss is the situation in the Cremisan Valley near Bethlehem. The valley, home to the Cremisan Monastery and its surrounding vineyards, has historically provided income and sustenance for the local Christian community, especially for the families that farm the land. The area is known for producing wine and olive oil, products that have long been tied to the religious and economic life of the community. However, Israeli authorities have sought to build the Separation Wall through the valley, effectively cutting off Christian farmers from their land. Despite protests, legal challenges, and international outcry—including from the Vatican—the construction of the Wall proceeded, leaving farmers with little to no access to the vineyards and olive groves that had sustained their families for generations. This loss of land has had devastating consequences, not only for the farmers who can no longer work their fields but also for the entire community that relied on the produce and income generated by these agricultural activities.

In Beit Jala, another predominantly Christian town near Bethlehem, local farmers have faced similar challenges. As Israeli settlements expand in the area, Christian farmers have found their lands either confiscated or rendered inaccessible by settlement infrastructure, security roads, and military restrictions. Many farmers who once worked large plots of land now find themselves unable to reach their fields due to military checkpoints, restricted zones, and physical barriers. Olive trees, which take years to mature and provide a vital source of income through the sale of olive oil, have been uprooted or destroyed to make way for settlement construction. For these farmers, the loss of their trees is not only an economic blow but also a personal and cultural tragedy, as olive farming has been a part of their way of life for centuries.

In the northern West Bank, Christian farmers in areas like Zababdeh and Burqin have also experienced the loss of agricultural land due to settlement expansion. These farmers, who primarily rely on olive cultivation, have seen their lands encroached upon by nearby settlements. As the boundaries of these settlements grow, Christian farmers find themselves hemmed in, with limited access to the land that has sustained their families for generations. In many cases, settlers have aggressively targeted these lands, destroying olive trees or preventing farmers from accessing their fields during critical harvest periods. With little recourse in the Israeli legal system, many of these farmers are left powerless to protect their livelihoods.

The economic impact of losing agricultural land has been severe for these Christian farmers. For many, agriculture was their primary source of income, and without access to their land, they have been left without a means to support their families. The loss of olive groves and vineyards has cut off not only their income from the sale of produce but also their ability to engage in traditional practices like olive oil production and winemaking. The economic void left by the loss of agriculture has forced many Christian families to leave their homes in search of better opportunities abroad, contributing to the ongoing emigration of Palestinian Christians from the Holy Land.

The destruction of agricultural land and the displacement of Christian farmers is not just an economic issue; it is also a cultural and spiritual one. For Palestinian Christians, the land is deeply connected to their identity and their religious heritage. Olive trees, in particular, hold significant symbolic and spiritual value, representing peace, endurance, and a connection to the land. The uprooting of these trees and the loss of farmland is not only a loss of income but also a severing of the ties that bind these communities to their ancestral land. The disappearance of Christian farmers from the land threatens the very existence of Christian culture and tradition in the region, as the community's connection to the land is eroded.

The lack of economic recourse for these farmers is further compounded by the Israeli legal system, which overwhelmingly favors settlers in land disputes. When Christian farmers attempt to challenge the confiscation of their land in Israeli courts, they face years of delays, legal fees, and bureaucratic hurdles, often with little hope of success. Even when rulings are made in favor of the farmers, enforcement is weak, and settlers frequently continue to occupy the land with the support of the Israeli military. This legal impunity leaves Christian farmers without any realistic path to reclaim their land or seek compensation for their losses.

The plight of Palestinian Christian farmers is emblematic of the broader economic and social challenges faced by the Christian community in the Holy Land. As settlement expansion continues to encroach on their land and livelihoods, many Christian families are left with no choice but to abandon their farms and seek a future elsewhere. The loss of agricultural land is not just a matter of economic survival; it is a threat to the very fabric of Christian life in Palestine. Without access to their land, these farmers and their families are losing not only their source of income but also their connection to the land that has been central to their identity for centuries.

Chapter 6: Between Walls and Checkpoints: The Daily Struggle of Christian Life

Living under occupation, Palestinian Christians face a daily reality shaped by the walls, checkpoints, and military presence that permeate their communities. The Israeli separation barriers, combined with a network of military checkpoints, have drastically altered the landscape of their lives, restricting access to essential services like schools, hospitals, and churches. These physical barriers not only hinder movement but also create a constant atmosphere of tension, fear, and isolation. For Palestinian Christians, these daily challenges are not just logistical inconveniences—they are deeply disruptive to their social, religious, and family lives. The impact of these barriers has forced Christian communities to navigate a complex and often hostile environment just to perform the most basic tasks, all while enduring the emotional strain of separation from loved ones and places of worship.

Life behind the barriers is marked by a sense of confinement. Israeli military checkpoints are a constant presence in the lives of Palestinian Christians, controlling their movement and dictating when and where they can travel. For many, even the simplest journeys—to school, to work, or to visit family—are fraught with uncertainty. Long lines, delays, and humiliating security checks are daily occurrences at these checkpoints. Christian families often find themselves stuck for hours, waiting to pass through, with no guarantee of how long they will be held or if they will be allowed to cross at all. This unpredictability has become a defining feature of life behind the barriers, as Palestinian Christians must adjust their schedules and daily routines to account for the possibility of being delayed or denied entry at any moment.

The impact of these barriers extends to every aspect of life. Schools, hospitals, and other essential services that would otherwise be easily accessible are now often located on the other side of checkpoints or walls. For children, the daily commute to school has become a daunting task, as they must pass through military checkpoints, where they are subjected to security screenings and delays. For those attending schools in Jerusalem or other cities divided by the Separation Wall, the journey can take hours each day, with the constant risk of being turned back or facing a sudden checkpoint closure. The psychological toll on children is profound, as they grow up in an environment where movement is restricted and fear is a constant companion.

Access to healthcare has also been severely restricted by the barriers. Palestinian Christians in need of medical attention often find that hospitals are located on the other side of checkpoints or walls, making it difficult to reach care in a timely manner. In emergency situations, delays at checkpoints can be life-threatening, as ambulances are frequently stopped and searched. For those with chronic health conditions, the constant uncertainty of whether they will be able to access the care they need adds an additional layer of stress and anxiety to their already difficult lives. The barriers, in effect, turn what should be basic rights—education and healthcare—into privileges that are difficult to attain.

The Separation Wall and checkpoints have also taken a deep emotional toll on Christian families, many of whom have been separated by these barriers. The Wall cuts through towns and neighborhoods, often dividing families from each other. Grandparents, parents, and children who once lived within walking distance of each other now find themselves on opposite sides of the Wall, unable to visit without passing through multiple military checkpoints. Family gatherings, holidays, and religious celebrations are all disrupted by the physical and bureaucratic obstacles imposed by the occupation. For Christian families, who place a strong emphasis on community and togetherness, this forced separation is a source of constant heartache.

The emotional strain of being separated from loved ones is compounded by the difficulty of accessing places of worship. The Separation Wall has cut off entire Christian communities from their churches, turning a simple act of attending a Sunday service into a logistical challenge. In cities like Bethlehem, where the Wall encircles the town, Christians must pass through military checkpoints just to attend church services. For some, this means waiting in line for hours, enduring security screenings, and facing the possibility of being turned away, all just to worship in their own churches. During major religious holidays such as Christmas and Easter, when Christians would traditionally gather in large numbers to celebrate, the barriers become even more restrictive, limiting access to holy sites like the Church of the Nativity in Bethlehem or the Church of the Holy Sepulchre in Jerusalem. For Palestinian Christians, these are not just inconveniences—they are deep spiritual wounds, as the physical barriers prevent them from fully practicing their faith and celebrating their religious traditions.

The Separation Wall has also isolated entire churches and religious communities. In some cases, congregations are cut off from their priests or pastors, as the clergy must navigate the same network of checkpoints and security barriers to reach their parishes. This isolation has weakened the bonds within Christian communities, as congregants find it more and more difficult to gather for regular worship, fellowship, and community activities. The presence of the Wall serves as a constant reminder of the division and disconnection that has been imposed on them, turning what were once vibrant religious communities into fragmented and isolated groups.

The barriers that define daily life for Palestinian Christians are not just physical; they are symbolic of the broader struggle for dignity, freedom, and a sense of normalcy in the face of occupation. Every checkpoint, every delay, and every restriction reinforces the sense of being trapped in a system that controls every aspect of their lives. For Christians living behind these walls, the struggle is not just about moving from one place to another—it is about maintaining their identity, their faith, and their connection to their families and communities in the face of overwhelming obstacles.

Despite these immense challenges, Palestinian Christians continue to resist the isolation and hardship imposed by the walls and checkpoints. Churches and community organizations provide support for those affected by the barriers, offering legal assistance, social services, and spiritual guidance. Families find ways to stay connected, even when physically separated, using technology and social networks to maintain their bonds. Yet, the daily struggle of life behind walls and checkpoints remains an enduring reality, one that weighs heavily on the future of Christian life in the Holy Land. Without meaningful change, the barriers that divide and isolate Palestinian Christians will continue to erode the social and spiritual fabric of their communities, threatening the survival of one of the world's oldest Christian populations.

Life Behind Barriers: The Daily Impact of Checkpoints and Military Presence on Palestinian Christians

FOR PALESTINIAN CHRISTIANS, life behind the Separation Wall and military checkpoints is a daily struggle marked by restrictions, delays, and uncertainty. The Israeli military presence throughout the West Bank, particularly around cities like Bethlehem, Beit Jala, and Jerusalem, has turned simple tasks—such as going to school, receiving medical care, or attending church—into complicated and often frustrating challenges. These barriers have not only disrupted the social and economic fabric of Palestinian Christian communities but have also taken a deep emotional and psychological toll on individuals and families. Every day, Palestinian Christians must navigate a maze of checkpoints, roadblocks, and military patrols that dictate when and where they can travel, cutting them off from essential services and isolating them from their places of worship.

One of the most immediate and visible impacts of Israeli checkpoints is the restriction on movement. For Palestinian Christians, access to schools, hospitals, and churches is often obstructed by a network of military checkpoints, which are designed to control and limit the movement of Palestinians. These checkpoints create long lines and delays, with individuals forced to wait hours to pass through, even when traveling short distances. The unpredictability of these delays means that many Palestinian Christians must factor in the possibility of being late or denied entry altogether, making it difficult to plan for work, education, or healthcare appointments.

Children and students are among the most affected by these movement restrictions. Many Palestinian Christian children must pass through military checkpoints just to get to school, a journey that should take minutes but often turns into an ordeal that can last hours. At the checkpoints, children are subjected to security checks and screenings, sometimes facing intimidation or harassment from soldiers. These daily encounters with military authority create an atmosphere of fear and anxiety for young students, who must contend with the uncertainty of whether they will make it to school on time—or at all. The disruption to their education is profound, as the checkpoints not only waste valuable time but also drain their mental energy and focus.

Access to healthcare is equally impacted by the presence of checkpoints and the Separation Wall. Palestinian Christians who need medical care often find that hospitals are located on the other side of the wall or beyond military checkpoints, making it difficult to reach critical services in a timely manner. In emergency situations, such as when someone is in need of urgent medical attention, delays at checkpoints can mean the difference between life and death. Ambulances are frequently stopped and searched, even when transporting critically ill patients, adding further delays to an already dire situation. For individuals with chronic health conditions who require regular medical treatment, the barriers create a constant burden, as they must plan their movements carefully to ensure they can access the care they need without unnecessary delays.

The separation from churches and places of worship is another profound consequence of life behind the barriers. For Palestinian Christians, faith and religious practice are central to their identity, and access to churches for worship and community events is essential to maintaining their spiritual lives. However, the Separation Wall and military checkpoints have physically divided Christian communities from their churches, making it difficult for congregants to attend regular services. In places like Bethlehem, where the Wall encircles the town, Christians must pass through military checkpoints just to attend Sunday services or celebrate religious holidays. For many, this means enduring long waits, security checks, and the constant fear of being turned away.

The situation is especially difficult during major religious holidays such as Christmas and Easter, when Christian pilgrims and local worshippers traditionally gather in large numbers to celebrate. The Church of the Nativity in Bethlehem and the Church of the Holy Sepulchre in Jerusalem are central to these celebrations, yet access to these holy sites is tightly controlled by Israeli authorities. Palestinian Christians from the West Bank are often required to apply for special permits to visit Jerusalem during these holidays, with no guarantee that they will be granted permission. For those who are denied permits, the inability to participate in these important religious events is a source of deep sorrow and frustration, as they are cut off from their most sacred traditions.

Beyond the physical barriers, the constant military presence creates an environment of intimidation and surveillance. The checkpoints are not just places where people are screened for security; they are also spaces where Palestinian Christians are reminded of their lack of freedom and the power dynamics that govern their daily lives. Soldiers armed with rifles stand watch over these crossings, controlling who can pass and when. The experience of being stopped, questioned, and searched on a daily basis fosters a sense of powerlessness and humiliation, as Palestinian Christians are treated as potential threats simply for trying to move about their own land.

The psychological and emotional toll of living behind barriers is significant. Palestinian Christians live with the constant awareness that their movements are restricted and that they are subject to the whims of military authority. This sense of confinement affects not only their physical freedom but also their mental and emotional well-being. The stress of navigating checkpoints, the fear of being denied access to essential services, and the frustration of being separated from family and community create an overwhelming sense of isolation. For many Palestinian Christians, the barriers are not just physical obstacles; they are symbols of a deeper, more profound form of oppression that limits their ability to live full and dignified lives.

Despite these challenges, Palestinian Christians continue to find ways to resist the isolation imposed by the barriers. Churches, community organizations, and local leaders work tirelessly to support those affected by the checkpoints, offering legal assistance, social services, and spiritual guidance. However, the daily struggle of life behind barriers remains a constant reminder of the broader political realities that shape their existence. As long as the checkpoints and military presence remain, Palestinian Christians will continue to face the hardship of restricted movement, limited access to services, and the emotional strain of life behind walls.

The Separation of Families: The Emotional Toll of Walls and Checkpoints on Christian Families

THE CONSTRUCTION OF the Israeli Separation Wall and the network of military checkpoints have not only divided land but also fractured families, creating deep emotional and psychological scars for Palestinian Christians. For many, the Wall has physically separated family members, making it difficult, if not impossible, to maintain close family ties. Christian families, who once lived within walking distance of each other, now find themselves on opposite sides of the Wall or forced to navigate multiple military checkpoints to meet. This enforced separation has taken an immense emotional toll, as the barriers disrupt family life, isolate loved ones, and prevent many from regularly attending church together. The psychological impact of these forced divisions is profound, as families face the pain of being kept apart by concrete walls and armed soldiers.

For Christian families, community and togetherness are central to their way of life. Traditionally, extended families lived close to each other, sharing daily life, celebrations, and support in times of need. However, the Separation Wall has literally cut through towns and neighborhoods, splitting families apart. Grandparents, parents, and children who once lived within the same community now find themselves on opposite sides of the barrier, unable to visit each other freely. Family gatherings, which once brought entire communities together for holidays, birthdays, and religious events, are now rare and difficult to organize. The Wall has turned these once-simple gatherings into complex logistical challenges, with family members needing to apply for permits, pass through checkpoints, and often endure long delays just to see one another.

The emotional toll of these separations is immense. For elderly family members, the inability to regularly see their children and grandchildren adds to the feelings of loneliness and isolation. Many elderly Christians, particularly those in East Jerusalem or the West Bank, find themselves confined to one side of the Wall, unable to visit family members who live just a few miles away. The barriers not only limit physical movement but also create emotional distance, as family bonds are strained by the constant challenges of navigating a divided landscape. For those with health issues, the separation is even more painful, as they are unable to rely on the care and support of their loved ones in times of need.

Younger generations are equally affected by these separations. Children who used to visit their grandparents, cousins, or aunts and uncles on weekends or after school now find such visits rare or nonexistent. The checkpoints, military patrols, and Separation Wall create a sense of fear and anxiety for children, who grow up in a world where family connections are disrupted by forces beyond their control. The emotional impact on children is profound, as they internalize the experience of separation and begin to view the barriers as an inescapable part of their lives. This early exposure to separation and confinement shapes their emotional development, leaving them with a sense of disconnection from both their families and their broader community.

The inability to regularly attend church as a family further deepens the emotional strain. For Palestinian Christians, religious life is a cornerstone of family and community identity, and attending church together is a vital part of their spiritual practice. However, the Separation Wall and military checkpoints have made it difficult for many families to worship together. In some cases, family members are separated from their churches, with parents on one side of the Wall and their children on the other. The logistics of passing through checkpoints, often involving long waits and security checks, make it hard for families to attend church services regularly, especially during major religious holidays such as Christmas and Easter.

The Wall has also cut off Christian families from sacred sites, such as the Church of the Nativity in Bethlehem and the Church of the Holy Sepulchre in Jerusalem. These sites hold deep religious significance for Christians, but access to them is tightly controlled by Israeli authorities. Many Palestinian Christians must apply for special permits to visit these holy sites, and even then, permits are frequently denied. For families who wish to make religious pilgrimages together, the barriers often make it impossible, creating a sense of spiritual disconnection and loss. The inability to visit these sacred places with family members, especially during important religious celebrations, is a source of deep sorrow for many Palestinian Christians.

The emotional toll of these separations is compounded by the constant uncertainty and stress of living in a divided and militarized environment. Families are never sure when they will be able to see each other again, as the rules governing permits and checkpoints can change without warning. The fear of being denied access or being stopped and questioned at a checkpoint creates a climate of anxiety that affects every aspect of family life. This uncertainty weighs heavily on Palestinian Christians, as they navigate the emotional complexities of maintaining family connections in a landscape that seems designed to keep them apart.

Despite these challenges, Palestinian Christian families continue to find ways to resist the separation imposed by the Wall and checkpoints. They use technology to stay in touch, relying on phone calls and video chats to maintain a sense of closeness despite the physical distance. Churches and community organizations also play a vital role in providing emotional and spiritual support, helping families cope with the pain of separation. However, the daily reality of being divided by walls and checkpoints remains a profound source of emotional strain, as families struggle to hold on to their relationships and their faith in the face of overwhelming obstacles.

The Separation Wall and military checkpoints have not only divided land but have also torn at the fabric of Palestinian Christian family life. The forced separation of loved ones, the difficulty of attending church together, and the constant uncertainty of navigating a militarized landscape have created deep emotional wounds that continue to fester. For Palestinian Christian families, the walls and checkpoints represent more than just physical barriers—they are symbols of a broader effort to fragment and isolate their communities, making it harder to maintain the close family bonds that have been central to their identity for generations.

Churches Behind Walls: The Separation of Christian Congregations from Their Places of Worship

THE ISRAELI SEPARATION Wall, along with a network of military checkpoints, has had a devastating impact on Palestinian Christian communities, many of whom are now cut off from their churches and places of worship. For these communities, attending religious services, a central aspect of their spiritual and communal life, has become an arduous and unpredictable journey. Congregations that once gathered freely for Sunday services, prayer meetings, and religious festivals now face the constant challenge of navigating barriers, checkpoints, and military restrictions just to enter their churches. The Wall, which was built under the pretext of security, has become a physical and symbolic divider between Christian communities and their faith, isolating them from the sacred spaces that have long been at the heart of their religious practices.

One of the most profound consequences of the Separation Wall has been its encirclement of key Christian towns like Bethlehem, Beit Jala, and other areas traditionally home to significant Christian populations. The Wall has physically cut these communities off from Jerusalem, where many of their most important churches, such as the Church of the Holy Sepulchre, are located. To visit these holy sites, Palestinian Christians are required to pass through multiple military checkpoints, where they are often subjected to long waits, security screenings, and the possibility of being denied entry altogether. The process of obtaining a permit to access Jerusalem, particularly for religious holidays like Easter and Christmas, is complex and unreliable, with many permits being denied without explanation. This has left entire Christian communities unable to freely visit the places of worship that are central to their faith.

In Bethlehem, the birthplace of Jesus Christ and home to the Church of the Nativity, the Separation Wall looms large, cutting off the town from its surrounding areas. For many Christians living in nearby villages or even within Bethlehem itself, attending services at the Church of the Nativity has become a difficult, and sometimes impossible, task. Military checkpoints block access to the church, forcing worshippers to navigate through a maze of barriers just to attend Sunday Mass or participate in religious celebrations. The Wall's presence casts a shadow over what should be a place of peace and reverence, turning the act of attending church into a struggle against the physical and political forces that seek to control every aspect of Palestinian life.

The physical separation of congregations from their churches is not just a logistical challenge; it is a profound spiritual wound. For Christians, gathering as a community to worship is a central tenet of their faith. It is in the church that they find solace, spiritual nourishment, and a sense of belonging. However, the Separation Wall and military checkpoints have disrupted this sense of community, isolating congregants from each other and from their places of worship. In many cases, priests and pastors who serve Christian congregations are themselves unable to regularly access their churches, as they too must pass through checkpoints or obtain permits. This has left some congregations without regular pastoral care, further weakening the spiritual bonds that hold these communities together.

The isolation caused by the Wall has also disrupted the rhythm of religious life in these communities. Important religious events, such as baptisms, weddings, and funerals, are now subject to the unpredictability of military control. Families who wish to gather for these sacred moments often find themselves separated by the Wall, with some members unable to obtain permits or pass through checkpoints in time for the ceremonies. The emotional toll of being cut off from these pivotal life events has been immense, as the Wall not only physically separates congregations from their churches but also prevents them from fully participating in the spiritual milestones that define their faith.

For those who manage to attend church, the experience is often marked by the presence of the Wall, a constant reminder of the barriers that divide their community. The journey to church, once a peaceful and routine part of life, is now fraught with tension and uncertainty. Worshippers must plan their day around the possibility of delays at checkpoints, often leaving hours earlier than necessary just to ensure they can arrive on time. For older congregants, the physical and emotional strain of passing through military checkpoints can be particularly difficult, as they are subjected to security searches and long waits that are both humiliating and exhausting.

The Separation Wall has not only isolated Christian communities from their churches but has also limited the ability of these churches to function as centers of social and charitable activity. Many churches in Palestine provide essential services to their communities, such as education, healthcare, and support for the poor. However, the barriers imposed by the Wall have made it increasingly difficult for churches to carry out these missions. Access to church-run schools and hospitals has been restricted, as students and patients must navigate checkpoints to receive the services they need. The logistical challenges of transporting goods and supplies to these institutions have further hampered their ability to operate, leaving many churches struggling to maintain their role as pillars of support in their communities.

Despite these overwhelming challenges, Palestinian Christians remain deeply committed to their faith and their churches. Congregations continue to gather for worship, even if it means enduring hours of waiting and uncertainty at checkpoints. Church leaders work tirelessly to serve their congregations, navigating the bureaucratic and physical obstacles that stand in their way. However, the toll of living behind walls and checkpoints is undeniable. The Separation Wall has not only created physical barriers but has also fractured the spiritual life of Palestinian Christian communities, turning their places of worship into sites of struggle and resistance.

The presence of the Wall around Christian towns and churches serves as a powerful symbol of the broader challenges faced by Palestinian Christians under occupation. It represents the isolation, fragmentation, and control that have come to define their daily lives. As long as the Wall remains, cutting off congregations from their churches, the spiritual and communal life of Palestinian Christians will continue to be under threat. Yet, in the face of these barriers, the resilience of these communities endures, as they hold on to their faith and their hope for a future where they can once again worship freely, without walls dividing them from their sacred spaces.

Chapter 7: Emigration: The Exodus of Christians from the Holy Land

The Holy Land, once the heart of Christianity, is witnessing the steady exodus of its Christian population. Over the past several decades, Palestinian Christians have been leaving their homeland at an alarming rate, driven by a combination of political oppression, economic hardship, and a sense of hopelessness under the ongoing Israeli occupation. Once vibrant communities that thrived in places like Bethlehem, Jerusalem, and Nazareth are now shrinking as more and more families choose to emigrate, seeking better opportunities and freedom abroad. This mass departure is not only a demographic crisis but also a profound loss for the region's Christian heritage, as the land where Christianity was born slowly becomes devoid of its native Christian population.

One of the primary reasons for this exodus is the pressure of living under Israeli occupation. Palestinian Christians, like their Muslim neighbors, face the daily challenges of restricted movement, military checkpoints, land confiscation, and a pervasive sense of insecurity. The Separation Wall, which cuts through Christian towns like Bethlehem, physically isolates communities and makes it difficult for Christians to access their places of worship, schools, and jobs. Constant military surveillance and the ever-present threat of violence from settlers add to the oppressive atmosphere. For many Christians, the relentless nature of this occupation has become unbearable, leaving them with no choice but to seek a life of freedom and safety elsewhere.

Economic hardship is another major factor contributing to the emigration of Palestinian Christians. The Israeli occupation has severely impacted the Palestinian economy, and Christian communities have not been spared. Land confiscations, settlement expansion, and restrictions on trade have devastated traditional industries such as farming, particularly olive cultivation, which has been a cornerstone of Christian livelihoods for centuries. The loss of farmland, combined with limited employment opportunities and rising poverty, has left many Christian families unable to support themselves. With few options for economic advancement in Palestine, many Christians are forced to emigrate in search of better opportunities in countries like the United States, Canada, and Europe.

The inability to live freely under the current conditions is also a key driver of emigration. Palestinian Christians are subject to the same discriminatory policies that affect the broader Palestinian population, including restrictions on movement, building permits, and access to resources. In East Jerusalem, for example, Christian families face the constant threat of losing their residency rights if they spend too much time outside the city, making it difficult to maintain homes and businesses. The systemic discrimination that permeates every aspect of life under occupation has created a sense of hopelessness, particularly among younger generations of Christians, who see little future for themselves in their homeland. For many, emigration feels like the only viable option to escape the stifling conditions imposed by the occupation.

The result of these pressures has been a dramatic decline in the Christian population in Palestine and Israel. Historically, Christians made up a significant portion of the population in cities like Bethlehem, where they once accounted for over 80 percent of the residents. Today, however, that number has dropped to around 12 percent, as thousands of Christians have left the area. In Jerusalem, the Christian population has similarly dwindled, with only a small fraction of the city's residents identifying as Christian. Across the Holy Land, the Christian community is now a tiny minority, struggling to maintain its presence in the face of ongoing emigration.

The impact of this population decline is profound, not only for the Christian community itself but also for the region's cultural and religious heritage. The Holy Land holds immense significance for Christians worldwide, as it is home to the most sacred sites in Christianity, including the Church of the Holy Sepulchre, the Church of the Nativity, and the Mount of Olives. These places, once vibrant with local Christian communities, are now increasingly devoid of the people who have lived and worshipped there for generations. The departure of Palestinian Christians threatens to turn the Holy Land into little more than a museum of Christian history, visited by tourists and pilgrims but no longer inhabited by a thriving Christian population.

Local churches are acutely aware of the crisis and are fighting to retain their congregations. Priests and pastors are working tirelessly to offer support and hope to their communities, despite the overwhelming challenges. Churches provide vital services such as education, healthcare, and social support, trying to alleviate some of the economic hardships that drive families to emigrate. In Bethlehem, Beit Jala, and other Christian towns, churches are actively engaging with their congregations, encouraging them to stay and maintain their roots in the Holy Land. However, the efforts of local churches are often overshadowed by the larger forces of occupation and economic instability, which continue to push Christians to seek a better life elsewhere.

Churches are not only facing the loss of their congregants but also struggling to maintain the physical and spiritual presence of Christianity in the Holy Land. With fewer parishioners, churches are finding it difficult to fund their operations, maintain their buildings, and keep their religious and social programs running. Many churches that once bustled with life are now half-empty, their pews filled mostly by elderly parishioners as younger generations emigrate in search of better opportunities. The decline in active congregations threatens the very existence of many churches, some of which may be forced to close their doors in the coming years if the exodus continues.

The exodus of Palestinian Christians is not just a local crisis; it is a global concern for the Christian faith. As the Christian population in the Holy Land dwindles, the global Christian community loses a vital connection to the birthplace of its faith. The churches and communities that have kept the Christian presence alive in Palestine for centuries are now on the brink of extinction, their numbers shrinking year by year. Without concerted efforts to address the root causes of this emigration—occupation, economic hardship, and discrimination—Christianity in the Holy Land risks becoming a relic of the past, remembered only in history books and tourist guides.

In the face of these challenges, Palestinian Christians continue to hold on to their faith and their heritage. Despite the hardships, many remain committed to their land and their churches, refusing to abandon the place where their faith was born. However, the pressures of occupation and economic despair are relentless, and without significant changes, the exodus of Christians from the Holy Land will likely continue, leaving behind only the echoes of a once-thriving community.

Fleeing Oppression: The Factors Driving Christian Emigration from Palestine

THE EXODUS OF CHRISTIANS from Palestine is a story of survival in the face of immense pressure, rooted in political oppression, economic hardship, and the overwhelming challenge of living under Israeli occupation. For many Palestinian Christians, life in the Holy Land has become increasingly unbearable as they contend with the harsh realities imposed by occupation forces and policies. These pressures have left Christians feeling trapped in a situation where they are unable to live freely, support their families, or practice their faith without fear or restriction. As a result, thousands of Christians have chosen to leave their homeland, seeking safety, stability, and opportunity elsewhere. This mass emigration is driven by three primary factors: the daily oppression of Israeli occupation, the economic challenges faced by Christian communities, and the loss of freedom that defines life under occupation.

One of the most significant reasons for Christian emigration is the pressure of living under Israeli occupation. Palestinian Christians, like their Muslim neighbors, experience the constant presence of Israeli military forces, who exert control over nearly every aspect of daily life. Checkpoints, roadblocks, and the Separation Wall restrict movement, making it difficult to travel between cities, visit family, or access essential services such as schools, hospitals, and churches. The constant surveillance and harassment by soldiers create a pervasive atmosphere of fear and insecurity. For Christians living in areas like Bethlehem and Jerusalem, the military presence is a daily reminder that their freedom is severely restricted, and the threat of violence or arrest looms large. This oppressive environment has driven many families to seek refuge in countries where they can live without fear of military intervention and control.

The physical barriers imposed by the Israeli occupation have also had a profound impact on the ability of Christians to maintain their religious practices. Many are cut off from their churches, particularly in Jerusalem, where the need for special permits to attend religious services creates an additional layer of frustration and alienation. The inability to freely worship, celebrate religious holidays, or even visit sacred Christian sites has left many feeling spiritually disconnected from the land that holds so much significance to their faith. This spiritual alienation, combined with the day-to-day realities of living under occupation, has pushed many to leave in search of a place where they can practice their religion freely.

Economic hardship is another major factor contributing to the emigration of Palestinian Christians. The Israeli occupation has crippled the Palestinian economy, and Christians have not been immune to its effects. Settlement expansion has led to the confiscation of Palestinian land, much of which has been historically owned by Christian families. This loss of land has particularly affected those who rely on agriculture, such as olive farmers, many of whom have seen their livelihoods destroyed as settlements encroach on their farmland. Additionally, the restrictions on movement make it difficult for Christians to engage in commerce or seek employment, as many jobs are located in areas that require crossing military checkpoints. The resulting economic instability has left many families struggling to make ends meet, with few opportunities for upward mobility.

The economic marginalization of Christians is further compounded by the lack of resources and government support. Israeli policies often favor Jewish settlers over Palestinians, and Christian communities are left to fend for themselves in an increasingly hostile economic environment. Schools, hospitals, and other essential institutions run by the church or local Christian organizations are often underfunded and face constant challenges in securing supplies due to the restrictions on movement and trade. Without access to stable employment, adequate resources, or the ability to expand their businesses, many Christians see emigration as the only viable option to secure a better future for their children.

Beyond political oppression and economic hardship, the loss of freedom under occupation has deeply impacted the decision to emigrate. Palestinian Christians live in a system that denies them basic rights and freedoms, making it impossible to build a life of dignity and security. The Israeli government's policies of land confiscation, settlement expansion, and restrictive residency laws disproportionately affect Palestinians, including Christians. For example, in East Jerusalem, Christian families are at constant risk of losing their residency rights if they are found to have lived outside the city for too long. This makes it difficult for Christians to travel or seek temporary work abroad without risking the permanent loss of their homes.

The sense of hopelessness is particularly acute among younger generations of Palestinian Christians. Many of them see no future in a land where opportunities are limited, mobility is restricted, and the political situation shows little sign of improvement. For these young Christians, the decision to emigrate is often motivated by the desire to escape a life of confinement and uncertainty. They seek a place where they can pursue education, careers, and personal freedom without the constant pressure of living under occupation. The drain of young talent and potential further weakens the remaining Christian communities, as those with the means to leave often choose to do so, leaving behind an aging population that struggles to maintain its cultural and religious heritage.

For many Palestinian Christians, emigration is not a choice taken lightly. It is a painful decision, driven by the realization that the land where their faith was born has become a place of oppression and hardship. Leaving behind their homes, churches, and communities is a heart-wrenching experience, but for those who have left, it is often seen as the only path to a life of freedom and dignity. As the pressure of occupation continues to mount, the exodus of Christians from Palestine shows no signs of slowing, raising concerns about the future of Christianity in the Holy Land. Without significant changes to the political and economic landscape, the Christian presence in Palestine may continue to dwindle, leaving behind only the traces of a once-thriving community.

The Dwindling Christian Population: A Threat to the Region's Christian Heritage

THE CHRISTIAN POPULATION in Palestine and Israel has been steadily declining for decades, a trend that threatens the rich Christian heritage of the region. Historically, Christians have played a significant role in the cultural, religious, and social life of the Holy Land, but the pressures of occupation, economic hardship, and emigration have drastically reduced their numbers. Today, Palestinian Christians make up only a small fraction of the population in their homeland, and this decline has profound implications for the preservation of Christian sites, traditions, and communities.

In the early 20th century, Christians made up approximately 10 percent of the population in Palestine. In cities like Bethlehem, Nazareth, and Jerusalem, Christian communities flourished, and Christian culture was an integral part of daily life. However, the ongoing Israeli-Palestinian conflict, combined with social and economic pressures, has led to a significant demographic shift. According to recent estimates, Christians now make up less than 2 percent of the population in the West Bank, Gaza, and Israel combined. In the West Bank, including Bethlehem, Christians currently represent about 1 to 2 percent of the population, a dramatic decline from the over 80 percent they once constituted in Bethlehem alone.

In Jerusalem, the Christian population has similarly diminished. At the beginning of the 20th century, Christians accounted for approximately 20 percent of the city's population. Today, they make up less than 2 percent. This dramatic decrease is particularly troubling in a city that is central to the Christian faith, home to some of the most important religious sites in the world, including the Church of the Holy Sepulchre. The shrinking Christian presence in Jerusalem is a stark reminder of how the region's demographic landscape is shifting, with profound consequences for the future of Christianity in its most sacred places.

One of the most alarming examples of this decline is in Bethlehem, the birthplace of Jesus Christ and a city of immense significance to Christians worldwide. Once a majority-Christian city, Bethlehem's Christian population has plummeted over the last few decades. Today, Christians make up just 12 percent of Bethlehem's population, down from over 80 percent in the mid-20th century. This decline is largely due to emigration, as Christian families leave in search of better economic opportunities and relief from the hardships of occupation.

The impact of this population decline is not just a demographic issue—it is also a cultural and religious one. The Christian heritage of the Holy Land is deeply intertwined with the presence of local Christian communities who have maintained and protected the region's most sacred sites for centuries. These communities are the caretakers of churches, monasteries, and holy places that are central to the Christian faith, such as the Church of the Nativity in Bethlehem and the Church of the Annunciation in Nazareth. As the Christian population dwindles, the ability of local Christians to preserve and protect these sites becomes increasingly precarious. The loss of a living Christian presence in these areas would not only diminish the region's rich religious diversity but also weaken the connection between Christians around the world and the birthplace of their faith.

The decline in the Christian population also has broader social and political implications. Christian communities in Palestine have long played a crucial role in fostering dialogue and cooperation between different religious groups, acting as a bridge between Muslims and Jews. The weakening of these communities threatens to erode this role, contributing to the further polarization of the region. Additionally, as Christian institutions such as schools, hospitals, and charitable organizations struggle to maintain their operations with fewer people and resources, the social fabric of Palestinian society becomes increasingly fragile.

While the global Christian community continues to visit the Holy Land as pilgrims and tourists, the local Christian population, which has lived and worshipped in the region for centuries, is disappearing. The dwindling number of Palestinian Christians raises concerns about the future of Christianity in the Holy Land. Without significant changes to the political, economic, and social conditions that drive emigration, the Christian presence in Palestine and Israel may become a distant memory, preserved only in historical records and monuments, rather than in the vibrant, living communities that once thrived in the region.

The loss of the Christian population is a tragedy for both the local communities and the global Christian faith. As more Christians leave the Holy Land, the connection between Christianity and its birthplace weakens. The continued decline threatens to transform the Holy Land from a living, breathing center of Christian faith into a museum of Christian history, visited by pilgrims but no longer inhabited by those who carry on the traditions and beliefs of their ancestors. Reversing this trend will require a concerted effort from the international community, including the support of churches, governments, and humanitarian organizations, to address the underlying causes of emigration and help Palestinian Christians remain in their homeland.

The disappearance of Palestinian Christians is a warning sign of the broader challenges facing the region. Without action to support the Christian communities that remain, the Holy Land risks losing an essential part of its religious and cultural identity, and with it, a vital link to the global Christian heritage.

Churches Fighting to Retain Congregations: The Struggle to Sustain Christian Communities in the Holy Land

AS THE CHRISTIAN POPULATION in Palestine continues to dwindle due to emigration, local churches find themselves in a constant battle to retain their congregations. The challenges of Israeli occupation, economic hardship, and restricted access to places of worship have forced many Palestinian Christians to leave the Holy Land in search of better opportunities abroad. For the churches that remain, maintaining active and vibrant congregations has become increasingly difficult as their numbers shrink year by year. Priests, pastors, and religious leaders are doing everything they can to keep their communities together, but they are fighting against a tide of emigration that threatens the survival of Christianity in the land where it was born.

One of the primary ways churches are attempting to retain their congregants is by providing critical social services that go beyond religious worship. Many churches in Palestine run schools, hospitals, and charitable organizations that serve both Christians and Muslims. These institutions offer education, healthcare, and financial support to families who are struggling under the weight of occupation and economic instability. By offering these essential services, churches hope to alleviate some of the hardships that drive families to emigrate, giving them reasons to stay and maintain their roots in the Holy Land. However, with fewer parishioners and limited resources, many of these institutions are facing significant financial difficulties, making it harder for churches to sustain their operations.

Churches also play a vital role in fostering a sense of community and cultural identity among Palestinian Christians. Religious leaders emphasize the importance of maintaining a Christian presence in the Holy Land, urging their congregants to stay despite the challenges they face. Through sermons, prayer services, and community events, churches seek to strengthen the bonds between families and remind them of their shared heritage and spiritual responsibility. These efforts are especially important during religious holidays such as Christmas and Easter, when churches organize large gatherings and celebrations that bring the community together. However, even these moments of unity are often overshadowed by the realities of occupation, as many Christians are cut off from their churches by the Separation Wall or are unable to attend services due to travel restrictions and military checkpoints.

Another major challenge facing local churches is the loss of younger generations, who are increasingly choosing to emigrate in search of better educational and career opportunities. For many young Palestinian Christians, the idea of building a future in a land where mobility is restricted and economic prospects are limited seems impossible. This has left churches with aging congregations, as fewer young people are available to take on leadership roles or participate in the day-to-day life of the church. Without the active involvement of younger generations, churches are finding it difficult to sustain their programs and activities, further contributing to the decline of Christian communities in the Holy Land.

In an effort to address the loss of young people, some churches have started youth outreach programs aimed at engaging the younger members of their congregations. These programs include religious education, social activities, and leadership training designed to keep young Christians connected to their faith and their community. Some churches have also partnered with international Christian organizations to offer scholarships and exchange programs, providing young people with opportunities for education and travel while encouraging them to return to Palestine and contribute to the local Christian community. However, despite these efforts, the lure of better opportunities abroad remains strong, and many young Christians continue to leave.

Financial difficulties are another major obstacle for local churches. With fewer parishioners to contribute donations, many churches are struggling to keep their doors open. The costs of maintaining church buildings, running social programs, and paying clergy and staff have become increasingly difficult to meet. In some cases, churches have had to reduce the number of services they offer or close certain programs due to a lack of funds. The decline in active congregations has also made it harder for churches to maintain their physical presence in the Holy Land. Historic churches, many of which have stood for centuries, are now in need of repairs and renovations that the local Christian community can no longer afford.

Despite these challenges, local churches remain committed to preserving the Christian presence in the Holy Land. Church leaders continue to advocate for the rights of Palestinian Christians, both locally and internationally, raising awareness about the struggles their communities face. Churches have also sought support from the global Christian community, appealing to international churches and organizations for financial assistance, solidarity, and advocacy. This support has been crucial in helping churches maintain their operations and continue serving their congregations, but it is not enough to fully counter the forces driving emigration.

For many Palestinian Christians, the decision to stay or leave is a deeply personal one, influenced by the desire for a better future for their children, the emotional toll of living under occupation, and the economic pressures they face. Local churches are doing everything they can to provide hope and support to those who remain, but they are fighting an uphill battle. As more Christians emigrate each year, the churches that remain are left with smaller, more fragile congregations, struggling to sustain the rich Christian heritage of the Holy Land.

The future of Christianity in the Holy Land is uncertain, but local churches are determined to continue their mission despite the many challenges they face. They remain a vital source of spiritual strength, community support, and cultural preservation for the Palestinian Christians who have chosen to stay. However, without significant changes to the political and economic conditions driving emigration, the Christian population in Palestine will likely continue to decline, leaving local churches with the daunting task of maintaining their presence in a land that is becoming increasingly devoid of its native Christian communities.

Chapter 8: Global Christian Support for Israel: Complicity Through Ignorance

Around the world, particularly in the United States and Europe, many Christians express strong support for the state of Israel. For some, this support is rooted in a deep religious connection to the Holy Land and a theological belief that Israel's existence fulfills biblical prophecy. However, this widespread backing of Israel often comes with little understanding of the profound impact it has on Palestinian Christians, who live under occupation and face ongoing hardships. As a result, many Western Christians, knowingly or unknowingly, become complicit in the oppression of their fellow believers in the Holy Land. The misguided support of Israel, driven by political, theological, and financial forces, often overlooks or even ignores the suffering of Palestinian Christians, who are being displaced, marginalized, and silenced in the land where Christianity was born.

One of the key issues is the widespread ignorance among Western Christians, particularly in the United States, about the realities on the ground in Israel and Palestine. Many Christian groups and denominations offer unequivocal support for Israel, viewing the modern state as an expression of biblical prophecy. This support is often bolstered by political movements that equate backing Israel with a commitment to religious principles. However, these Christians are often unaware of how Israeli policies—such as settlement expansion, land confiscation, and military occupation—directly harm Palestinian Christians. The very communities that have lived in the Holy Land for centuries, maintaining Christian traditions and sacred sites, are now facing displacement, economic hardship, and social isolation.

This ignorance is particularly stark in countries like the United States, where Christian Zionism plays a significant role in shaping political attitudes toward Israel. Christian Zionism is a theological and political movement that views the creation and continued support of the state of Israel as a fulfillment of biblical prophecy. Many adherents believe that supporting Israel is a religious duty, and they provide both financial and political backing to the Israeli state without questioning the broader implications for the people living in the region, including Palestinian Christians. For Christian Zionists, the focus on Israel as a divinely-ordained nation often overrides concerns about justice, human rights, and the well-being of Palestinians, including those who share their Christian faith.

The role of Christian Zionism in fueling this one-sided support for Israel is significant. Organizations and churches that subscribe to this theology donate millions of dollars each year to Israeli causes, including settlements in the West Bank, which are built on confiscated Palestinian land. These financial contributions help sustain the very policies that lead to the displacement of Palestinian Christians and the erosion of their communities. Meanwhile, Christian Zionists frequently lobby their governments to adopt pro-Israel policies, further marginalizing Palestinians in the political discourse. This narrow focus on supporting Israel, based on an apocalyptic reading of scripture, leaves little room for acknowledging the suffering of Palestinian Christians, who are often seen as collateral damage in a larger divine plan.

This theological framework creates a dangerous dynamic where Palestinian Christians are effectively invisible in the global Christian conversation. The irony is striking: while Western Christians send money and political support to Israel, Palestinian Christians, who live in the very places that many of these Christians consider sacred, are struggling to survive. Churches are being isolated by the Separation Wall, Christian families are being displaced by settlement expansion, and the Christian population in the Holy Land is dwindling. Yet, the plight of these Palestinian Christians is often ignored by the very global Christian organizations that claim to care deeply about the Holy Land.

Specific instances of this neglect can be seen in the actions of some prominent Christian organizations and leaders who vocally support Israel while failing to advocate for Palestinian Christians. For example, large evangelical organizations in the U.S. frequently sponsor tours to Israel, encouraging Christians to visit biblical sites while simultaneously celebrating Israeli military achievements and political policies. These tours often ignore or gloss over the reality of Palestinian life under occupation, focusing solely on the Jewish-Israeli narrative. The Palestinian Christian experience is either omitted or relegated to a footnote, further marginalizing a community that is already struggling to maintain its presence in the Holy Land.

Moreover, many global Christian leaders have remained silent when it comes to speaking out against the injustices faced by Palestinian Christians. While there are Christian organizations that advocate for peace and justice in the region, they are often overshadowed by larger and more influential groups that either actively support Israeli policies or refrain from criticizing them. This silence, whether intentional or not, sends a message that the suffering of Palestinian Christians is not a priority. As a result, the voices of Palestinian Christians are drowned out, and their pleas for help and solidarity go unanswered.

The consequences of this global complicity are devastating for Palestinian Christians. As more Christians around the world support Israel without fully understanding the impact on their fellow believers in Palestine, the situation for these communities continues to deteriorate. Churches are left with dwindling congregations, young people are emigrating in search of better opportunities, and the

Christian presence in the Holy Land is gradually disappearing. The very survival of these ancient Christian communities is now at risk, and without a shift in how global Christians engage with the issue, the Holy Land may soon become a place where the Christian population is nothing more than a distant memory.

It is crucial for global Christians to reconsider their support for Israel and recognize the complex realities faced by Palestinian Christians. Blindly supporting the Israeli state without acknowledging the harm being done to Palestinian communities, including Christians, is not only unjust but also undermines the very values that Christianity espouses: justice, compassion, and solidarity with the oppressed. It is time for Christian organizations and individuals to listen to the voices of Palestinian Christians, to stand with them in their struggle, and to advocate for a just and lasting peace in the Holy Land that respects the rights and dignity of all people, regardless of religion or nationality.

The Misguided Support of Western Christians: Ignoring the Consequences for Palestinian Christians

IN THE UNITED STATES and Europe, a significant number of Christians express strong support for the state of Israel, often without fully understanding the complex consequences that this has for their Palestinian Christian brothers and sisters. Many of these Christians are motivated by religious, political, or historical reasons, believing that supporting Israel is both a theological imperative and a moral obligation. However, this widespread backing often comes at the expense of the Palestinian Christian community, which suffers under the policies and occupation practices of the Israeli state. The uncritical and one-sided support of Israel by Western Christians not only overlooks the plight of Palestinian Christians but also contributes to the erosion of Christian presence in the Holy Land.

Much of the support for Israel in the West stems from a religious belief that the modern state of Israel is a fulfillment of biblical prophecy. For many evangelical Christians, particularly in the United States, the existence of Israel is seen as a necessary precursor to the second coming of Christ. This belief, rooted in Christian Zionism, has led to a robust political and financial backing of Israel. These Christians view the support of Israel as a religious duty, often ignoring the human rights violations, land confiscations, and systemic oppression faced by Palestinians, including Christians, in the occupied territories. The focus on Israel as a divine mandate blinds many to the suffering of Palestinian Christians, who are caught in the crossfire of policies that privilege one group over another.

The theological narrative that drives much of this support overlooks the reality that Palestinian Christians have lived in the Holy Land for centuries, long before the establishment of the modern state of Israel. These Christians are the living descendants of the earliest followers of Jesus, maintaining churches, traditions, and communities in the places where Christianity itself was born. However, the expansion of Israeli settlements, the construction of the Separation Wall, and the military occupation of Palestinian lands have all placed immense pressure on these communities. As Christian families are displaced, their lands confiscated, and their access to churches restricted, the very existence of these ancient communities is threatened. Yet, Western Christians who support Israel often fail to acknowledge or understand these consequences.

This misguided support is particularly pronounced in the United States, where many churches and Christian organizations provide financial and political backing to Israel without questioning its impact on Palestinian Christians. Donations to Israeli causes, including those that fund settlement expansion, are common among evangelical churches, and many of these churches organize tours to Israel that celebrate the state's achievements while ignoring the struggles of

Palestinian Christians. These tours often present a one-sided narrative, focusing on biblical sites and the modern Jewish state while bypassing Palestinian communities entirely. As a result, Western Christians return home with a distorted understanding of the region, unaware of the daily hardships faced by their fellow Christians living under occupation.

The political influence of Christian Zionism in the U.S. has also played a role in shaping government policy toward Israel. Christian Zionist groups frequently lobby for policies that support Israeli interests, such as continued military aid and diplomatic backing, while remaining silent on issues related to Palestinian rights. This political support has further marginalized Palestinian Christians, whose voices are drowned out by the powerful alliance between American evangelical groups and pro-Israel lobbies. The result is a political landscape in which the suffering of Palestinian Christians is overlooked, and their legitimate grievances are ignored in favor of an unwavering commitment to Israel's political and territorial goals.

In Europe, while the situation is somewhat different, many Christians still offer uncritical support for Israel, often out of a sense of historical guilt or solidarity with the Jewish people. The horrors of the Holocaust and centuries of Christian anti-Semitism have led to a widespread belief that supporting Israel is a moral obligation. While addressing the historical wrongs committed against the Jewish people is important, it should not come at the expense of Palestinian Christians, who are now bearing the brunt of policies that disenfranchise and displace them. The Christian commitment to justice and human dignity must extend to all people, including Palestinians who are suffering under occupation.

The failure of Western Christians to understand the full impact of their support for Israel on Palestinian Christians is not just a matter of ignorance—it is also a moral failure. By focusing exclusively on the needs and desires of the Israeli state, many Western Christians are complicit in the suffering of their fellow believers in Palestine. The continued financial, political, and theological support for Israel, without acknowledging the rights of Palestinians, contributes to the erosion of Christian communities in the Holy Land. As more Palestinian Christians are forced to emigrate due to economic hardship, political oppression, and social isolation, the Christian presence in the land where the faith was born is slowly disappearing.

Western Christians who are serious about their faith and their commitment to justice must reexamine their support for Israel in light of the consequences for Palestinian Christians. Blind allegiance to the Israeli state, motivated by theological or political concerns, cannot justify the ongoing suffering of those who are being displaced from their homes, denied access to their churches, and stripped of their land. A more nuanced and compassionate approach is needed—one that recognizes the rights and dignity of all people in the region, including Palestinian Christians, and advocates for a just and lasting peace that respects the needs of all communities.

The time has come for Western Christians to open their eyes to the reality of life for Palestinian Christians and to reconsider the ways in which their support for Israel may be contributing to the oppression of their fellow believers. Rather than offering unconditional support for one side of the conflict, Christians must seek a more balanced and informed approach—one that aligns with the core values of their faith: love, justice, and solidarity with the oppressed. Only then can they truly stand with their Christian brothers and sisters in the Holy Land, working together toward a future where all people can live in peace and dignity.

The Role of Christian Zionism: Driving Political and Financial Support for Israel at the Expense of Palestinian Christians

CHRISTIAN ZIONISM IS a theological and political movement that has become a significant force in shaping the support of Israel among many Christians, particularly in the United States. This movement is rooted in the belief that the establishment and continued existence of the state of Israel is a fulfillment of biblical prophecy, and that supporting Israel is a divine mandate for Christians. While this ideology has driven substantial political and financial backing for Israel, it has also come at a great cost to Palestinian Christians, whose suffering is often ignored or overshadowed by the overwhelming focus on supporting Israel's interests.

At the heart of Christian Zionist theology is the interpretation of certain biblical passages, particularly those in the Old Testament, which are seen as foretelling the return of the Jewish people to the Holy Land and the reestablishment of Israel as a nation. For Christian Zionists, the founding of the modern state of Israel in 1948 is viewed as a direct fulfillment of these prophecies, and many believe that Israel's existence is a key step in God's divine plan for the world. This theology places a heavy emphasis on the idea that supporting Israel is not just a political choice but a religious obligation for Christians, who see their backing of Israel as aligning with God's will.

This theological framework has led to widespread political and financial support for Israel, particularly among evangelical Christians in the United States. Organizations and churches that subscribe to Christian Zionism raise millions of dollars each year to support various Israeli causes, including the development of settlements in the West Bank, which are often built on confiscated Palestinian land. These settlements, which are illegal under international law, have led to the displacement of Palestinian families, including Christians, who are losing their homes and livelihoods. However, Christian Zionist supporters frequently overlook or dismiss these consequences, focusing instead on their belief that they are helping to fulfill biblical prophecy.

Christian Zionism also has a powerful influence on American politics, as many of its adherents actively lobby for U.S. policies that favor Israel. Christian Zionist organizations like Christians United for Israel (CUFI) have become major players in Washington, advocating for continued U.S. military aid to Israel, opposition to Palestinian statehood, and support for Israeli settlement expansion. These lobbying efforts have a profound impact on U.S. foreign policy, often leading to decisions that prioritize Israel's security and territorial ambitions while sidelining the rights and aspirations of Palestinians, including the Palestinian Christian community.

One of the central tenets of Christian Zionism is the belief that the land of Israel was divinely promised to the Jewish people and that no other group has a legitimate claim to it. This belief has led many Christian Zionists to turn a blind eye to the plight of Palestinian Christians, who have lived in the region for centuries. The focus on Israel's biblical entitlement to the land means that the suffering of Palestinians—whether Muslim or Christian—is often minimized or ignored. For Christian Zionists, the political and territorial conflict in the region is seen through a narrow theological lens, where the displacement and oppression of Palestinians are regarded as either necessary or irrelevant to the larger divine plan.

The financial backing of Israel by Christian Zionists has also had tangible consequences for Palestinian Christians. Many Christian Zionist organizations directly fund projects in Israeli settlements, providing financial support for housing, infrastructure, and social services that are often denied to Palestinians living under occupation. These donations help sustain the expansion of settlements, which encroach on Palestinian land and further marginalize Palestinian communities. In some cases, Christian Zionist groups even fund the construction of roads and schools that serve only Israeli settlers, leaving Palestinian Christians and Muslims cut off from essential services. The economic support for settlements exacerbates the inequalities and injustices faced by Palestinians, while reinforcing the political status quo that allows Israel to continue its occupation of the West Bank.

One of the most troubling aspects of Christian Zionism is its silence on the suffering of Palestinian Christians. While Christian Zionist leaders and organizations are vocal in their support for Israel, they rarely, if ever, speak out about the challenges faced by Palestinian Christians living under Israeli occupation. The voices of Palestinian Christians, who are experiencing displacement, economic hardship, and restrictions on their religious freedom, are often marginalized in the Christian Zionist narrative. This silence is particularly striking given that these Palestinian Christians are the descendants of the earliest followers of Christ, living in the land where Christianity was born. Yet, their struggles are largely ignored in favor of a theological focus on supporting Israel at all costs.

In some cases, Christian Zionist leaders have even suggested that Palestinian Christians should accept their suffering as part of God's plan. This interpretation effectively dismisses the legitimate grievances of Palestinian Christians, including the loss of their homes, land, and freedom, and frames their plight as a necessary sacrifice for the fulfillment of biblical prophecy. This attitude not only undermines the efforts of Palestinian Christians to seek justice and dignity in their homeland but also alienates them from the global Christian community, which should be advocating for their rights and supporting their struggle.

The political influence of Christian Zionism extends beyond financial donations and lobbying. It has also shaped the way that Israel is presented to the broader Christian world, particularly through media and educational initiatives. Christian Zionist organizations frequently sponsor tours to Israel, bringing groups of Christians to visit biblical sites while promoting a pro-Israel narrative. These tours often highlight the achievements of the modern Israeli state while downplaying or ignoring the hardships faced by Palestinians. The result is a one-sided understanding of the region, where Israel is seen as the fulfillment of God's promise and Palestinians, including Christians, are viewed as obstacles to that fulfillment.

The impact of Christian Zionism on the relationship between global Christians and Palestinian Christians is profound. By focusing exclusively on supporting Israel, Christian Zionists have contributed to the marginalization of Palestinian Christians, who often feel abandoned by their fellow believers in the West. This theological and political movement has created a stark divide within global Christianity, where the voices and experiences of Palestinian Christians are silenced in favor of a narrative that prioritizes Israel's geopolitical interests. For many Palestinian Christians, this sense of abandonment is deeply painful, as they struggle to maintain their presence in the land of their faith while being ignored by the very global Christian community that should be standing in solidarity with them.

Christian Zionism's unwavering support for Israel, driven by a narrow interpretation of biblical prophecy, has profound consequences for the people of the Holy Land, particularly Palestinian Christians. By focusing on the theological imperative to support Israel, Christian Zionists have overlooked the suffering of Palestinian communities, whose lives have been upended by occupation and settlement expansion. The political and financial backing provided by Christian Zionists has reinforced the systems of oppression that keep Palestinian Christians marginalized, while their voices go unheard. It is time for global Christians to reevaluate this theology and recognize the need for a more just and balanced approach—one that acknowledges the rights and dignity of all people in the Holy Land, including the Palestinian Christian community.

Ignoring the Suffering of Fellow Christians: Global Christian Organizations' Failure to Support Palestinian Christians

IN RECENT DECADES, many global Christian organizations, particularly those with strong ties to Christian Zionism, have actively supported Israeli interests while failing to address or acknowledge the suffering of Palestinian Christians. These organizations often champion Israel's political and military policies, donate significant funds to Israeli causes, and lobby governments in favor of Israel, all while neglecting the hardships faced by their fellow Christians in Palestine. This disregard for Palestinian Christians—who are living under occupation, facing displacement, and experiencing severe restrictions on their religious freedoms—has left a deep sense of abandonment and isolation within these ancient communities. Several specific instances highlight how global Christian organizations have not only overlooked but actively contributed to this neglect.

One glaring example is the widespread support of Israeli settlement expansion by Christian Zionist organizations. Many of these organizations, particularly in the United States, raise millions of dollars each year to fund the construction of settlements in the West Bank. These settlements are often built on land confiscated from Palestinians, including Christian families, who are forcibly displaced as their homes and farms are taken over for settlement development. Despite the clear impact these settlements have on the Palestinian Christian community, many Christian organizations continue to provide financial and political backing for these projects, often under the guise of supporting biblical prophecy. For instance, large evangelical organizations like Christians United for Israel (CUFI) have repeatedly advocated for the expansion of Israeli settlements, ignoring the fact that these actions contribute directly to the marginalization and displacement of Palestinian Christians.

Another example is the silence of many global Christian leaders and institutions in the face of the humanitarian crisis faced by Palestinian Christians. While these organizations often speak out on issues of global Christian persecution, such as the oppression of Christians in the Middle East or Africa, they rarely address the specific challenges faced by Palestinian Christians living under Israeli occupation. The daily realities of checkpoints, restricted access to holy sites, and the confiscation of Christian-owned land are often absent from the public discourse of these organizations. When Palestinian Christian leaders have appealed to their global counterparts for solidarity and support, these pleas have frequently gone unanswered, leaving them to face their struggles alone.

For example, during the construction of the Israeli Separation Wall in the early 2000s, many Palestinian Christian leaders voiced strong opposition to the Wall's route, which cut through Christian communities, separating families from their churches and holy sites. The Wall's construction in places like Bethlehem and Beit Jala physically isolated Christian communities, making it difficult for them to access their places of worship and even attend religious services. Despite the clear and detrimental impact on Christian life in the region, many global Christian organizations remained silent, offering little support to their Palestinian brothers and sisters. Instead, much of the international Christian focus remained on supporting Israel's security narrative, failing to acknowledge how the Wall was further marginalizing the local Christian population.

The actions of some Christian organizations during major religious holidays also reveal a disturbing neglect of Palestinian Christians. Every year, Christian Zionist organizations organize large-scale tours and pilgrimages to Israel, bringing thousands of Christians from around the world to visit biblical sites in Jerusalem and other parts of Israel. These tours often include visits to major Christian holy sites, such as the Church of the Holy Sepulchre and the Church of the Nativity.

However, these tours frequently overlook the Palestinian Christian communities who live near these sites, failing to engage with local Christians or support their struggling communities. Moreover, these tours often uncritically promote a pro-Israel narrative, ignoring the challenges faced by Palestinian Christians and reinforcing the political and social status quo that keeps them marginalized.

Perhaps one of the most notable examples of global Christian organizations actively supporting Israeli interests while ignoring Palestinian Christians is the role of lobbying in the United States. Christian Zionist organizations like CUFI have played a key role in shaping U.S. foreign policy toward Israel, advocating for continued military aid and political backing for Israeli policies, including the expansion of settlements and the annexation of Palestinian land. While these organizations claim to support Israel out of a sense of biblical duty, their lobbying efforts have consistently disregarded the impact of these policies on Palestinian Christians. By prioritizing Israel's political agenda, these Christian groups have actively contributed to the very policies that are driving Palestinian Christians out of their homeland, without offering any meaningful support to those suffering under these conditions.

Another specific instance where global Christian organizations have failed to support Palestinian Christians is their silence on the issue of access to holy sites. For many Palestinian Christians, the Israeli occupation has made it increasingly difficult to access some of Christianity's most sacred places, including the Church of the Nativity in Bethlehem and the Church of the Holy Sepulchre in Jerusalem. The Separation Wall, military checkpoints, and permit requirements make it nearly impossible for many Palestinian Christians to attend religious services or celebrate major religious holidays at these sites. Yet, global Christian organizations that routinely organize pilgrimages to these very sites have largely remained silent on the issue. Rather than advocating for the rights of Palestinian Christians to freely access their holy places, these organizations continue to focus on promoting tourism and financial support for Israel, while ignoring the barriers faced by the local Christian population.

In contrast to this silence, some Palestinian Christian leaders have been vocal in their criticism of these global Christian organizations, calling out their complicity in the suffering of Palestinian Christians. In 2009, a group of Palestinian Christian leaders issued the Kairos Palestine document, a powerful statement that called on global Christians to reconsider their support for Israel in light of the ongoing occupation and oppression of Palestinians. The document appealed to Christians around the world to stand in solidarity with Palestinian Christians and to advocate for a just peace in the Holy Land. However, the response from many global Christian organizations was muted, with some outright rejecting the call for solidarity and others continuing to focus their attention on supporting Israel.

The failure of global Christian organizations to support Palestinian Christians, while actively advocating for Israeli interests, has had devastating consequences for the Christian presence in the Holy Land. As more Palestinian Christians are displaced and forced to emigrate, the Christian population in the region continues to dwindle. Churches that have stood for centuries are now facing the threat of closure, and the Christian community is becoming increasingly isolated and marginalized. Without meaningful support from the global Christian community, the very existence of Christianity in the land where it was born is at risk.

It is time for global Christian organizations to acknowledge the suffering of their fellow Christians in Palestine and to reconsider their uncritical support for Israel. Rather than prioritizing political and financial backing for Israeli interests, these organizations must stand in solidarity with Palestinian Christians, advocating for their rights, their freedom, and their survival in the Holy Land. Only then can the global

Christian community truly live up to its values of justice, compassion, and solidarity with the oppressed.

Chapter 9: Weaponizing Faith: Israel's Use of Christian Pilgrimages for Political Gain

Christian pilgrimages to the Holy Land have been a longstanding tradition, drawing millions of believers from around the world to visit the sacred sites where Jesus lived, preached, and was crucified. For many, the opportunity to walk in the footsteps of Christ is a deeply spiritual experience, one that strengthens their faith and connects them to the biblical narrative. However, in recent years, Israel has increasingly capitalized on this religious devotion, using Christian pilgrimage tourism as a political tool to bolster its image on the global stage while systematically oppressing the local Palestinian Christian population. By promoting a carefully curated image of the Holy Land to international pilgrims, Israel is able to divert attention away from the harsh realities of life under occupation, particularly for the Palestinian Christians who live in the very places these pilgrims come to visit.

The politics of pilgrimage in Israel are deeply intertwined with the state's broader political goals. Christian pilgrims, particularly those from the United States and Europe, are welcomed with open arms by Israeli authorities, who see them as both a source of economic profit and political support. Pilgrims are often taken on carefully guided tours that highlight the biblical significance of various sites while avoiding the contentious political landscape that surrounds them. These tours typically focus on the positive aspects of Israel's role in preserving Christian holy sites, while downplaying or entirely ignoring the ongoing occupation of Palestinian territories and the suffering of the local Christian population. By presenting a sanitized version of the Holy Land, Israel is able to win over the hearts and minds of Christian pilgrims, many of whom return home with a one-sided view of the region that reinforces their political support for Israel.

This selective narrative is part of Israel's broader strategy to promote itself as the guardian of the "Holy Land." The Israeli government actively markets the country as a safe and welcoming destination for Christian pilgrims, highlighting its role in maintaining access to Christian holy sites such as the Church of the Nativity in Bethlehem and the Church of the Holy Sepulchre in Jerusalem. Promotional materials often emphasize the biblical connections of the land, portraying Israel as a modern-day protector of Christian heritage. However, this carefully constructed image stands in stark contrast to the lived reality of Palestinian Christians, who face daily struggles under Israeli occupation. The same government that welcomes international pilgrims is responsible for the construction of settlements on confiscated Palestinian land, the restriction of movement through checkpoints, and the separation of Christian communities from their places of worship.

For Palestinian Christians, the Israeli occupation has made it increasingly difficult to access the very holy sites that pilgrims visit. The Separation Wall, military checkpoints, and permit requirements have turned what should be short journeys to church into lengthy and often impossible endeavors. In cities like Bethlehem, where the Church of the Nativity is located, Palestinian Christians are frequently cut off from their own churches, forced to pass through checkpoints to attend Sunday services or religious holidays. Meanwhile, Christian pilgrims are able to move freely, visiting these same sites without experiencing the barriers that define everyday life for Palestinian Christians. The stark contrast between the treatment of international pilgrims and local Christians reveals the underlying political agenda: while Israel is eager to present itself as a friend of global Christianity, it systematically oppresses the indigenous Christian population.

One of the most troubling aspects of Israel's use of Christian pilgrimages for political gain is the economic exploitation of religious tourism. Christian pilgrims are a significant source of revenue for Israel, contributing millions of dollars annually to the tourism industry. Hotels, restaurants, tour companies, and souvenir shops all benefit from the influx of Christian tourists, many of whom are unaware of the challenges faced by the local Palestinian Christian population. The financial benefits of pilgrimage tourism are largely concentrated in Israeli businesses and institutions, with very little of the revenue reaching Palestinian communities. In Bethlehem, for example, most Christian pilgrims visit the Church of the Nativity but stay in Israeli-owned hotels, eat in Israeli-owned restaurants, and purchase souvenirs from Israeli-owned shops, leaving the local Palestinian economy struggling to survive.

This economic dynamic is particularly damaging for Palestinian Christians, whose communities are already suffering under the weight of occupation. Many Palestinian Christian businesses, particularly those in the tourism industry, have been severely impacted by the restrictions on movement and the dominance of Israeli-controlled tourism infrastructure. Christian-owned hotels and restaurants in Bethlehem, Jerusalem, and other key pilgrimage sites struggle to compete with their Israeli counterparts, which benefit from government support and easier access to resources. As a result, Palestinian Christians are increasingly marginalized within the tourism industry, even as Christian pilgrims flock to visit the holy sites that define their faith.

Israel's ability to profit from Christian pilgrimages is directly tied to the ignorance of many pilgrims about the political and social realities of the region. Most Christian tourists are unaware of the challenges faced by Palestinian Christians, as their tours rarely engage with local communities or address the complexities of life under occupation. Instead, pilgrims are presented with a narrative that focuses on the biblical significance of the land while avoiding the uncomfortable truths of modern-day Israel-Palestine. This selective storytelling not only shields pilgrims from the reality of Palestinian suffering but also reinforces the perception that Israel is a benevolent caretaker of Christian holy sites, deserving of continued financial and political support.

The exploitation of Christian pilgrimage tourism for political and economic gain highlights the deep disconnect between Israel's treatment of international Christians and its treatment of Palestinian Christians. While Israel welcomes Christian pilgrims with open arms, it systematically oppresses the indigenous Christian population, cutting them off from their land, their holy sites, and their livelihoods. This two-faced approach to Christian engagement allows Israel to present itself as a champion of religious freedom while actively contributing to the decline of Christianity in the Holy Land.

For the global Christian community, it is essential to recognize the political agenda behind Israel's promotion of pilgrimage tourism and to understand the impact that this has on Palestinian Christians. Christian pilgrims must be aware that their visits, while spiritually significant, are also being used to support a political narrative that ignores the suffering of their fellow Christians. By engaging more deeply with the realities of life for Palestinian Christians and supporting local businesses and communities during their pilgrimages, global Christians can begin to counterbalance the harmful effects of Israel's political exploitation of faith. Only through a more informed and compassionate approach to pilgrimage can Christians help preserve the Christian heritage of the Holy Land for future generations, while standing in solidarity with those who are most affected by the ongoing conflict.

The Politics of Pilgrimage: Israel's Use of Christian Tourism to Mask the Oppression of Local Christians

ISRAEL HAS LONG RECOGNIZED the powerful draw of the Holy Land for Christians around the world. Millions of believers journey to Israel each year, eager to visit biblical sites and connect with the land where Christianity was born. For many, these pilgrimages are deeply spiritual, providing a tangible link to their faith. However, behind the scenes, Israel has strategically used Christian pilgrimage tourism as a political tool. While welcoming international Christian tourists with open arms, Israel simultaneously oppresses the local Palestinian Christian population, creating a stark divide between the image it projects to the world and the realities of life on the ground for those who call the Holy Land home.

The welcoming nature of Israel's approach to Christian pilgrims is part of a carefully constructed narrative designed to bolster Israel's global image. By presenting itself as the guardian of Christian holy sites, Israel seeks to strengthen its ties with Christian communities around the world, particularly in the United States and Europe. This relationship is not only religious but also political, as Israel knows that securing the support of global Christians can translate into diplomatic and financial backing. Pilgrimage tourism is central to this strategy, as it allows Israel to showcase its role as a protector of the Holy Land while cultivating goodwill among visiting Christians. Pilgrims return home with positive experiences of their time in Israel, often unaware of the broader political context, and their support for Israel's policies is strengthened as a result.

However, this carefully curated image obscures the reality of Israel's treatment of its local Christian population, particularly the Palestinian Christians who live in the West Bank, Gaza, and East Jerusalem. While international Christian tourists are free to move about and visit holy sites, Palestinian Christians face severe restrictions on their movement. The Separation Wall, military checkpoints, and Israeli permit systems make it difficult—if not impossible—for many Palestinian Christians to access their churches and religious sites. For instance, while tourists visit the Church of the Nativity in Bethlehem with relative ease, local Palestinian Christians may struggle to attend Sunday Mass or religious festivals due to the checkpoints that separate their homes from the church. This duality—welcoming Christian tourists while oppressing local Christians—reveals how Israel uses pilgrimage tourism as a tool of soft power to distract from the hardships imposed on the indigenous Christian population.

The Israeli government has also strategically marketed itself to global Christians by promoting the idea that it is preserving and protecting Christian holy sites. This narrative portrays Israel as a safe and stable country, where Christian pilgrims can explore the land of the Bible without fear. By emphasizing its role as a protector of these sacred places, Israel strengthens its political connections with Christian leaders and communities abroad. Yet, this narrative is misleading. While Israel may protect the physical structures of churches, it does little to support the local Christian communities who maintain these sites. In fact, many of Israel's policies directly harm these communities, including the confiscation of Christian-owned land, the expansion of settlements in Christian-majority areas, and the imposition of harsh restrictions on movement and access to religious sites.

This political use of pilgrimage tourism serves another important function for Israel: it helps to divert attention from the ongoing occupation of Palestinian territories. Tourists who visit Israel on pilgrimage are often shielded from the realities of life under occupation. Their tours rarely include visits to Palestinian villages or conversations with local Palestinian Christians, leaving them with a skewed understanding of the region. Instead, many Christian tourists are taken on carefully guided tours that emphasize the biblical significance of the land while avoiding any mention of the political tensions that shape daily life for Palestinians. By controlling the narrative, Israel is able to maintain its image as a friendly and welcoming destination, even as it enforces policies that oppress the Palestinian people, including Palestinian Christians.

Moreover, Israel's use of Christian pilgrimage as a political tool extends beyond simply welcoming tourists. It actively seeks to build alliances with Christian Zionist groups, particularly in the United States, who view the state of Israel as the fulfillment of biblical prophecy. These groups organize large pilgrimage tours to Israel, bringing thousands of Christians each year to visit the Holy Land. These tours often reinforce a one-sided narrative that celebrates Israel's role in biblical history while ignoring the present-day struggles of Palestinian Christians. As a result, Christian Zionist pilgrims return home with a strong pro-Israel stance, which in turn influences their political and financial support for Israel. This support often comes at the expense of advocating for justice and human rights for Palestinian Christians, who are left out of the narrative entirely.

While Christian pilgrims may leave Israel with a deeper connection to their faith, the political implications of their visits are significant. By focusing on the spiritual experience of pilgrimage, Israel is able to mask the reality of its occupation and human rights abuses. The economic benefits of Christian tourism further entrench this dynamic, as Israel profits from the influx of tourists while local Palestinian businesses and communities are sidelined. In cities like Bethlehem, where Christian pilgrimage is a major industry, Palestinian Christian business owners struggle to compete with Israeli-owned hotels, restaurants, and tour companies that dominate the tourism market. The profits generated by Christian pilgrimages flow largely into the Israeli economy, while Palestinian Christians receive little of the economic benefits despite being the custodians of many of the holy sites that draw tourists in the first place.

In essence, the politics of pilgrimage in Israel reveal a deep hypocrisy. Israel's embrace of Christian pilgrims is not motivated solely by a desire to share the Holy Land with the faithful; it is a calculated strategy designed to garner political support, economic profit, and international legitimacy. By controlling the narrative and hiding the oppression of Palestinian Christians behind a facade of religious tourism, Israel is able to strengthen its global alliances while continuing to enforce policies that harm the very communities that should be at the heart of Christian pilgrimage.

For global Christians, understanding the politics behind pilgrimage is essential. It is important to recognize that while Israel welcomes Christian tourists, it simultaneously enforces policies that marginalize the local Christian population. Christian pilgrims must look beyond the surface of their spiritual journeys and engage with the political realities of the region, listening to the voices of Palestinian Christians who are struggling to maintain their presence in the land where their faith was born. By doing so, they can contribute to a more just and balanced understanding of the Holy Land, one that acknowledges both the spiritual significance of the region and the need for justice and peace for all its inhabitants.

Promoting the 'Holy Land' Image: Israel's Marketing to Global Christians vs. the Reality for Palestinian Christians

ISRAEL HAS EXPERTLY crafted and promoted its image as the guardian of the 'Holy Land,' drawing millions of Christian pilgrims annually who seek a spiritual connection to the land of the Bible. By marketing itself to global Christian communities as a safe, welcoming, and hospitable destination for believers, Israel fosters a narrative of peace and religious coexistence. This carefully constructed image is a powerful tool in securing the political and financial support of

Christians around the world, particularly in countries like the United States and Europe. However, this polished image contrasts starkly with the harsh realities faced by Palestinian Christians, who live under occupation and face daily challenges that are hidden from the majority of Christian tourists.

Israel's marketing strategy focuses heavily on its role as the protector of Christian holy sites, emphasizing its stewardship of key religious landmarks such as the Church of the Holy Sepulchre in Jerusalem and the Church of the Nativity in Bethlehem. These sites, which are central to Christian history and spirituality, are presented as being well-maintained and accessible, thanks to Israel's governance. Israel's tourism materials highlight the seamless blend of ancient history and modern infrastructure, portraying a nation that respects and values its Christian heritage. The message is clear: Israel is not only a homeland for Jews but also a safe haven for Christians who wish to experience the land where their faith was born.

The images and narratives presented to global Christians are carefully curated to evoke a sense of biblical awe and reverence. Pilgrims are encouraged to explore sites such as the Sea of Galilee, the Mount of Olives, and the Jordan River, all places rich with religious symbolism. The emphasis is on spiritual renewal and connection, and many Christian tourists return home with positive impressions of Israel as a country that not only shares their values but actively protects the sacred spaces that define their faith. This image of Israel as a friendly, benevolent nation is reinforced by the country's partnership with Christian tour operators, churches, and religious organizations that promote pilgrimage trips to the Holy Land.

However, this idealized version of Israel is incomplete and misleading. It conceals the ongoing occupation and systematic oppression faced by Palestinian Christians, who are native to the very land that is being marketed as a spiritual destination. While international Christian tourists are able to visit these sites with relative ease, the local Palestinian Christian population faces numerous barriers. Checkpoints, travel permits, and the Separation Wall severely limit the freedom of movement for Palestinian Christians, many of whom are cut off from their own holy sites. For example, while pilgrims from around the world freely visit the Church of the Nativity in Bethlehem, Palestinian Christians who live just a few miles away often struggle to gain access due to Israeli-imposed travel restrictions.

This stark contrast between the experience of Christian tourists and that of Palestinian Christians highlights the deep inequality at the heart of Israel's tourism industry. The image of the 'Holy Land' that Israel promotes is one of religious harmony and preservation, but the reality is that local Christian communities are being systematically marginalized. Land confiscations, settlement expansions, and discriminatory zoning laws have made it increasingly difficult for Palestinian Christians to remain in the land of their ancestors. Many have been forced to emigrate due to economic hardship, and the Christian population in Palestine has steadily declined as a result. Yet, this reality is rarely, if ever, mentioned in the glossy brochures and promotional videos that target global Christian tourists.

Israel's marketing campaign also fails to address the broader political context of the Israeli-Palestinian conflict. The occupation of Palestinian territories, the expansion of settlements on confiscated land, and the military presence in areas with significant Christian populations are all omitted from the narrative that is presented to Christian pilgrims. The focus remains solely on the spiritual significance of the land, with little to no acknowledgment of the struggles faced by Palestinian Christians. This omission allows Israel to maintain its carefully cultivated image as a protector of religious freedom while actively contributing to the marginalization of one of the world's oldest Christian communities.

Furthermore, Israel's tourism industry is structured in such a way that the financial benefits of Christian pilgrimage flow primarily into

Israeli businesses, with little reaching the Palestinian Christian community. Israeli-owned hotels, restaurants, and tour companies dominate the market, leaving Palestinian-owned businesses struggling to compete. In cities like Bethlehem, where Christian tourism should be a major source of revenue, the local Palestinian economy is often sidelined by Israeli control over tourism infrastructure. This economic disparity further exacerbates the challenges faced by Palestinian Christians, who are increasingly dependent on international aid and church support to survive.

The selective marketing of the 'Holy Land' also serves to reinforce political support for Israel among global Christian communities. By presenting itself as the protector of Christian holy sites, Israel cultivates a narrative that aligns with the theological beliefs of many Christians, particularly those who subscribe to Christian Zionism. This narrative helps to solidify the political and financial backing of Christian groups that view the modern state of Israel as a fulfillment of biblical prophecy. As a result, many global Christians are encouraged to support Israel's political and military policies without fully understanding the impact these policies have on Palestinian Christians.

Ultimately, Israel's promotion of the 'Holy Land' image is a powerful tool in shaping global perceptions of the country. It allows Israel to present itself as a beacon of religious freedom and security while masking the harsh realities of life for Palestinian Christians under occupation. For Christian tourists, the experience of pilgrimage is often deeply spiritual and transformative, but it is important to recognize that this experience is shaped by a narrative that omits the suffering of local Christians. To fully understand the complexities of the Holy Land, global Christians must look beyond the carefully curated image and engage with the lived realities of Palestinian Christians who are struggling to maintain their presence in the land where their faith began.

Profiting from the Ignorance of Pilgrims: Israel's Economic Gains from Christian Tourism Amid Local Christian Struggles

CHRISTIAN PILGRIMAGES to the Holy Land are a major source of revenue for Israel, with millions of pilgrims traveling annually to visit the sacred sites connected to their faith. For many Christians, these trips are a once-in-a-lifetime opportunity to walk where Jesus walked, visit places of biblical significance, and deepen their spiritual connection to their faith. However, behind this spiritual journey lies a deeper, often unseen reality: Israel's tourism industry reaps significant economic benefits from Christian pilgrimages, while the Palestinian Christian communities that maintain and protect many of these holy sites struggle under the weight of occupation and economic marginalization. By capitalizing on the ignorance of many Christian tourists about the political and social dynamics of the region, Israel profits handsomely while offering little support to the local Christians who are the custodians of these sacred places.

The economic structure of Israel's tourism industry is designed to ensure that the bulk of the financial benefits from Christian pilgrimages flow directly into Israeli businesses. From the moment pilgrims arrive in Israel, they are directed toward Israeli-owned hotels, restaurants, tour companies, and souvenir shops. These businesses are located primarily in cities like Jerusalem, Tel Aviv, and Haifa, where Israeli control over tourism infrastructure is most pronounced. Pilgrims are often unaware of the economic disparity between Israeli-owned businesses and those run by Palestinian Christians, particularly in areas like Bethlehem and the West Bank. As a result, the vast majority of the money spent by Christian tourists never reaches the Palestinian Christian communities that are most in need of economic support.

Bethlehem, one of the most important pilgrimage destinations for Christians, provides a striking example of this economic imbalance. The city is home to the Church of the Nativity, the birthplace of Jesus Christ, and attracts thousands of pilgrims each year. However, despite the religious and cultural significance of Bethlehem to Christians worldwide, the local Palestinian Christian community has seen little of the financial benefits from this influx of tourism. Israeli tour companies often structure pilgrimages in such a way that pilgrims visit the Church of the Nativity briefly before returning to Israeli-controlled areas to spend their money. As a result, Palestinian Christian-owned hotels, restaurants, and shops in Bethlehem struggle to survive, even as the city remains one of the most visited Christian pilgrimage sites in the world.

This economic marginalization is compounded by the restrictions placed on Palestinian businesses by the Israeli government. Palestinian Christian entrepreneurs in Bethlehem and other cities face significant challenges in accessing permits, licenses, and resources needed to operate their businesses. The Separation Wall, which surrounds much of Bethlehem, not only physically isolates the city from Jerusalem but also hinders the movement of goods and people. Palestinian Christian business owners are forced to navigate a complex and often discriminatory system of permits and checkpoints, making it difficult for them to compete with their Israeli counterparts. Meanwhile, Israeli businesses enjoy the benefits of government subsidies, modern infrastructure, and unrestricted access to key tourist destinations.

The ignorance of many Christian pilgrims about these dynamics allows Israel to maintain control over the narrative and the profits. Most Christian tourists are unaware of the daily struggles faced by Palestinian Christians, as their tours are designed to focus solely on the spiritual and historical aspects of the pilgrimage. Tour operators often avoid discussing the political and social realities of life under occupation, leaving pilgrims with a one-sided view of the region. As a result, Christian tourists return home with a positive image of Israel as a protector of Christian holy sites, without realizing that their pilgrimage dollars are contributing to an economic system that marginalizes the very people who have maintained these sites for centuries.

In addition to profiting from the tourism industry, Israel uses Christian pilgrimages as a tool to further its political agenda. By promoting itself as the guardian of Christian holy sites, Israel strengthens its relationships with global Christian communities, particularly in the United States and Europe. The financial support that comes from Christian tourists and pro-Israel Christian organizations helps to reinforce Israel's political standing, while the struggles of Palestinian Christians are conveniently overlooked. This political and economic support allows Israel to continue its policies of settlement expansion, land confiscation, and occupation, all of which further marginalize Palestinian Christians.

The impact of this economic disparity on Palestinian Christian communities is profound. Many Palestinian Christians have been forced to leave their homeland due to a lack of economic opportunities, exacerbated by the restrictions placed on their businesses and the unequal distribution of tourism revenue. The Christian population in the West Bank, including Bethlehem, has steadily declined as a result of emigration, with families seeking better opportunities abroad. This demographic shift threatens the very existence of Christianity in the land where it was born, as the local Christian population continues to dwindle in the face of economic and political challenges.

The exploitation of Christian pilgrimages for economic gain is not limited to Israel's control over the tourism industry. Christian Zionist organizations, which organize large pilgrimage tours to Israel, also play a role in reinforcing the economic imbalance. These organizations often partner with Israeli businesses, further directing the flow of tourism dollars away from Palestinian Christian communities. Moreover, the theological framework of Christian Zionism, which views the state of Israel as a fulfillment of biblical prophecy, encourages Christian pilgrims to support Israeli causes financially. This support often comes in the form of donations to Israeli settlements, which are built on confiscated Palestinian land, further deepening the economic and social hardships faced by Palestinian Christians.

The failure to engage with Palestinian Christian communities during pilgrimages is a missed opportunity for global Christians to support their brothers and sisters in faith. By directing their spending toward Israeli businesses and ignoring the economic struggles of local Christians, pilgrims inadvertently contribute to the very system that is driving Palestinian Christians out of their homeland. This disconnect between the spiritual experience of pilgrimage and the reality of life for Palestinian Christians underscores the need for greater awareness and action within the global Christian community.

Christian pilgrims who seek a deeper connection to their faith through visits to the Holy Land must also seek a deeper understanding of the social, political, and economic realities of the region. By supporting Palestinian Christian businesses, engaging with local communities, and advocating for justice and equality, pilgrims can play a role in preserving the Christian presence in the Holy Land. It is essential for global Christians to recognize that their pilgrimage dollars have the power to either support or undermine the very communities that have kept the Christian faith alive in the region for centuries. Without a more informed and ethical approach to Christian tourism, the economic and political systems that marginalize Palestinian Christians will continue to thrive, to the detriment of the Christian heritage of the Holy Land.

Chapter 10: Media Silence: How the Western Press Ignores the Struggle of Palestinian Christians

In the complex and often polarized landscape of the Israeli-Palestinian conflict, one group consistently finds its voice drowned out or entirely ignored: Palestinian Christians. Despite their deep roots in the Holy Land and their enduring presence in the region, the struggles faced by Palestinian Christians under Israeli occupation receive scant attention from Western media outlets. Coverage of the conflict tends to focus on the broader Jewish-Muslim dynamics, framing the narrative in terms of religious and territorial disputes between these two groups, while the unique challenges experienced by Palestinian Christians are left largely unreported. This media silence not only marginalizes their plight but also perpetuates a misunderstanding of the conflict, erasing a vital part of the Holy Land's Christian heritage.

One of the main reasons for this media silence is the prioritization of broader political narratives that overshadow the experiences of Palestinian Christians. Western media outlets, particularly in the United States and Europe, often frame the Israeli-Palestinian conflict in simplistic terms—focusing on the violence between Jewish Israelis and Muslim Palestinians. This binary framework leaves little room for the complexities of Palestinian Christian experiences, despite the fact that these communities face many of the same struggles as their Muslim neighbors, including land confiscation, restrictions on movement, and economic marginalization. The result is that the voices of Palestinian

Christians are rarely heard, and their experiences are overshadowed by the larger geopolitical focus.

This underreporting is further complicated by political bias in Western media coverage, which is often influenced by the political interests of powerful governments. Israel enjoys strong diplomatic and military support from Western nations, particularly the United States, and this relationship shapes how the conflict is portrayed in the media. Coverage often emphasizes Israel's security concerns, portraying it as a democratic state surrounded by hostile neighbors. This narrative, which aligns with the foreign policy objectives of many Western governments, leads to an imbalance in reporting that downplays or ignores the impact of Israeli policies on Palestinian communities, including Christians. Palestinian Christians, who are caught between the Israeli state and the broader Palestinian struggle for rights, are often overlooked as their unique stories do not fit neatly into the dominant political narrative.

Additionally, Western media outlets often avoid covering the oppression of Palestinian Christians out of fear of being accused of bias against Israel. Criticizing Israeli policies, particularly those related to settlement expansion, military occupation, or the treatment of Palestinian Christians, can lead to accusations of anti-Semitism or unbalanced reporting. This fear of backlash leads many media organizations to either downplay the stories of Palestinian Christians or avoid reporting on them altogether, contributing to the ongoing erasure of their voices. As a result, the daily challenges faced by Palestinian Christians—such as restrictions on accessing their holy sites, the loss of Christian-owned land to Israeli settlers, and the emigration crisis caused by economic hardship—rarely make headlines.

The impact of this media silence is profound. Without regular coverage and visibility, the struggles of Palestinian Christians remain unknown to much of the world, particularly to global Christian communities who might otherwise offer support. Many Western

Christians are unaware of the fact that their brothers and sisters in the faith are facing significant challenges in the land where Christianity was born. This ignorance not only isolates Palestinian Christians but also perpetuates their marginalization within the broader narrative of the conflict. By focusing exclusively on the Jewish-Muslim dynamic, Western media effectively erases the Christian dimension of the struggle, leaving the global Christian community uninformed about the hardships faced by Palestinian Christians.

In contrast to the minimal coverage in mainstream media, independent and alternative media outlets have occasionally highlighted the struggles of Palestinian Christians. Reports from non-governmental organizations, human rights groups, and religious advocacy groups have documented the challenges faced by these communities, from land confiscation to the decline of Christian populations in historically significant areas like Bethlehem and Jerusalem. However, these reports often struggle to reach a broad audience, as they lack the visibility and influence of major Western media organizations. Without the amplification of these voices by mainstream media, the stories of Palestinian Christians remain largely confined to niche publications, limiting their ability to generate global awareness and action.

The silence of Western media is not just an issue of underreporting but also of misrepresentation. When Palestinian Christians do appear in media narratives, their struggles are often subsumed under the broader Palestinian experience, with little distinction made between the unique challenges faced by Christian communities. This lack of differentiation ignores the specific pressures placed on Palestinian Christians, such as the emigration crisis driven by economic and political instability, and the loss of access to their religious sites. It also overlooks the role that Palestinian Christians have historically played as mediators and bridge-builders within Palestinian society, contributing to interfaith dialogue and fostering cooperation between Muslims and

Christians. By failing to highlight these contributions, the media perpetuates a narrative that excludes a vital part of Palestinian history and culture.

Breaking this media silence is crucial for ensuring that the voices of Palestinian Christians are heard and their struggles recognized. Increased coverage of their experiences could lead to greater international support for their communities and help to preserve the Christian presence in the Holy Land. Moreover, by acknowledging the unique challenges faced by Palestinian Christians, the media can provide a more accurate and nuanced understanding of the Israeli-Palestinian conflict, one that includes all of the region's religious and cultural dimensions.

There is a growing need for journalists, editors, and media organizations to challenge the existing narratives that dominate coverage of the Israeli-Palestinian conflict. This means seeking out the stories of Palestinian Christians, interviewing local leaders, and exploring the ways in which Israeli policies specifically impact these communities. It also means amplifying the voices of Palestinian Christian activists, clergy, and laypeople who are working to defend their rights and preserve their communities in the face of ongoing challenges. By doing so, the media can help to break the cycle of silence and bring much-needed attention to the plight of Palestinian Christians.

Ultimately, the Western press has a responsibility to provide balanced, comprehensive coverage of the Israeli-Palestinian conflict—coverage that includes the experiences of all communities affected by the occupation, including Palestinian Christians. Without this broader perspective, the true complexity of the conflict is obscured, and the suffering of Palestinian Christians remains invisible. It is time for the media to give Palestinian Christians the attention they deserve and ensure that their voices are no longer silenced in the story of the Holy Land.

The Role of Western Media in Silencing the Christian Struggle

WESTERN MEDIA PLAYS a significant role in shaping global perceptions of the Israeli-Palestinian conflict, but it often falls short when it comes to representing the full complexity of the situation. One of the most glaring omissions in mainstream coverage is the underreporting and misrepresentation of the plight of Palestinian Christians. While media outlets frequently focus on the broader Jewish-Muslim dynamics of the conflict, the unique struggles faced by the Christian population in Palestine are often overlooked or reduced to a minor subplot in the larger narrative. This silence not only marginalizes Palestinian Christians but also distorts the reality of life under occupation, leaving global audiences with an incomplete understanding of the conflict.

The tendency of Western media to focus predominantly on Jewish-Muslim tensions stems in part from the way the Israeli-Palestinian conflict is framed for international audiences. The conflict is often presented as a binary struggle between Jewish Israelis and Muslim Palestinians, a framing that simplifies the situation but fails to capture the diverse religious and cultural makeup of the region. This reductionist approach leaves little room for the experiences of Palestinian Christians, who are caught in the crossfire of the occupation and face many of the same challenges as their Muslim neighbors, including land confiscation, restricted access to religious sites, and economic hardship.

In focusing on Jewish-Muslim dynamics, Western media effectively silences the Christian voice in the conflict, even though Palestinian Christians have played a significant role in the history and culture of the Holy Land. As one of the oldest Christian communities in the world, Palestinian Christians have maintained churches, schools, and religious traditions in the land where Christianity was born. Yet, their presence and contributions are often invisible in Western media narratives, which tend to highlight religious tensions between Jews and Muslims while ignoring the struggles of Christian Palestinians who face unique challenges under Israeli occupation.

This media silence is particularly evident in coverage of key events related to the conflict. For example, when news outlets report on the construction of the Israeli Separation Wall, the focus is typically on how it affects Muslim Palestinians in terms of security, movement, and access to resources. Little attention is given to the fact that the Wall also cuts through Christian communities, separating Palestinian Christians from their churches, schools, and holy sites. In Bethlehem, the birthplace of Jesus, the Wall has isolated Palestinian Christians from their neighboring communities, yet this aspect of the story is rarely covered in detail by Western media. Instead, the broader narrative of security and territorial disputes dominates the discourse, leaving the Christian experience largely unreported.

One of the reasons for this underreporting is the political bias that shapes media coverage of the Israeli-Palestinian conflict. Many Western countries, particularly the United States, maintain strong political and military alliances with Israel, and this relationship influences how the conflict is portrayed in the media. Coverage that emphasizes Israel's security concerns or presents the conflict as a battle between Jewish and Muslim populations aligns with the foreign policy objectives of these governments. As a result, stories that might complicate this narrative—such as the oppression of Palestinian Christians—are often downplayed or ignored. The struggles of Palestinian Christians do not fit neatly into the dominant political narrative, making them less likely to be covered by mainstream media outlets that are sensitive to the political dynamics surrounding Israel.

Furthermore, the fear of being accused of anti-Semitism or bias against Israel also contributes to the media's reluctance to cover the struggles of Palestinian Christians. Journalists and news organizations may avoid reporting on stories that highlight the negative impact of

Israeli policies on Christian communities out of concern that they will face backlash or accusations of being unfairly critical of Israel. This fear of criticism leads to self-censorship, where important stories about the Christian population are left untold, further marginalizing Palestinian Christians in the global conversation.

When Palestinian Christians do appear in Western media, their struggles are often generalized and subsumed into the broader Palestinian experience, with little recognition of the specific challenges they face. For example, while both Christian and Muslim Palestinians suffer from the effects of land confiscation and settlement expansion, Palestinian Christians face additional pressures related to their religious identity and access to holy sites. Churches in the West Bank and East Jerusalem have been targeted for settlement projects, and Christian-owned lands have been confiscated for the construction of Israeli settlements, yet these stories rarely make it into the mainstream media. By failing to highlight the distinct struggles of Palestinian Christians, the media perpetuates a narrative that erases their unique experiences and contributions.

The consequences of this media silence are far-reaching. Without adequate coverage, the global Christian community remains largely unaware of the hardships faced by their fellow Christians in the Holy Land. Many Western Christians, particularly in the United States and Europe, are unaware of the fact that Palestinian Christians are being displaced from their homes, losing access to their holy sites, and facing economic hardships due to Israeli occupation. This ignorance prevents international Christian organizations from fully engaging with the issue and offering the support that Palestinian Christians desperately need. The absence of media coverage also means that Palestinian Christian voices are excluded from the broader discussions about peace and justice in the region, further isolating these communities.

Breaking this silence is essential for achieving a more comprehensive and just understanding of the Israeli-Palestinian conflict. Western media must expand its coverage to include the voices and experiences of Palestinian Christians, who are an integral part of the region's history and culture. Journalists should seek out stories that highlight the specific challenges faced by Christian communities under occupation, from the loss of land and property to the restrictions on religious freedom. By giving Palestinian Christians the platform they deserve, the media can provide a more accurate and nuanced picture of the conflict, one that reflects the diversity of the people living in the Holy Land.

Increased media attention to the plight of Palestinian Christians can also help to mobilize global support for these communities. When the struggles of Palestinian Christians are made visible, international organizations, religious institutions, and advocacy groups can begin to take action to address their needs and advocate for their rights. This, in turn, can help to preserve the Christian presence in the Holy Land and ensure that Palestinian Christians are not erased from the region's future.

Ultimately, the Western media has a responsibility to provide balanced and comprehensive coverage of the Israeli-Palestinian conflict. This means moving beyond the simplistic framing of the conflict as a Jewish-Muslim struggle and acknowledging the experiences of all communities affected by the occupation, including Palestinian Christians. By doing so, the media can help to break the silence that has long surrounded the Christian struggle in Palestine and ensure that their voices are heard in the global conversation about peace and justice in the Holy Land.

Political Bias in Coverage: How Political Interests Shape the Narrative and Erase Christian Voices from the Conflict

POLITICAL BIAS PLAYS a significant role in shaping the media's portrayal of the Israeli-Palestinian conflict, often leading to a one-dimensional narrative that focuses on the Jewish-Israeli and Muslim-Palestinian struggle. This biased coverage largely erases the experiences and voices of Palestinian Christians, despite their deep historical and cultural ties to the Holy Land. The political interests of Western nations, particularly those with strong alliances with Israel, influence how the conflict is reported, often prioritizing narratives that align with their foreign policy goals. As a result, the unique challenges faced by Palestinian Christians under occupation are sidelined, further marginalizing an already vulnerable population.

One of the primary ways political bias shapes media coverage is through the framing of the conflict in terms that align with the strategic interests of Western governments, especially the United States and its European allies. These nations maintain close political, economic, and military ties with Israel, viewing it as a key ally in the Middle East. As a result, the media often emphasizes Israel's security concerns and portrays the conflict as a battle between a democratic state and its hostile neighbors. This framing naturally lends itself to focusing on the Jewish-Muslim dynamic, highlighting the tensions between Israeli Jews and Palestinian Muslims, while downplaying the experiences of Palestinian Christians, who do not fit neatly into this binary narrative.

The close diplomatic and military relationship between Israel and Western governments also influences the language and tone of media coverage. For instance, when reporting on Israeli policies such as settlement expansion or military actions, the media tends to frame these actions in terms of Israel's right to self-defense or as responses to terrorism. This framing obscures the impact of these policies on Palestinian Christians, many of whom are displaced from their homes or face restrictions on their religious freedoms. The political interests of Western nations in supporting Israel make it less likely for mainstream media outlets to critically examine these policies or highlight the specific ways they affect Christian communities in the occupied territories.

In addition to shaping the broader narrative, political bias also manifests in the selective reporting of events. Stories that align with the dominant political narrative—such as rocket attacks from Gaza or the security concerns of Israeli citizens—are more likely to receive prominent coverage. Conversely, stories about the displacement of Palestinian Christian families, the confiscation of Christian-owned land, or the struggles of Christian churches under occupation are often underreported or ignored entirely. This selective reporting reinforces the idea that the Israeli-Palestinian conflict is primarily a Jewish-Muslim issue, leaving little room for the complexities of the Christian experience in the Holy Land.

The political interests of Western governments also lead to the erasure of Christian voices from the conflict through the marginalization of Palestinian Christian leaders and activists in the media. Palestinian Christian clergy and community leaders, who often advocate for peace and justice, are rarely featured in mainstream news outlets. When they do speak out about the impact of Israeli policies on their communities, their voices are often drowned out by the more dominant narratives that focus on Jewish and Muslim perspectives. This erasure not only limits the visibility of Palestinian Christians but also prevents their concerns from being heard by a global audience, particularly the global Christian community, which could offer support and solidarity.

Moreover, the fear of political backlash or accusations of bias against Israel also plays a role in how the media covers the conflict.

Journalists and media organizations that report on the negative impact of Israeli policies on Palestinian Christians risk being labeled as anti-Israel or even anti-Semitic. This fear leads to self-censorship, where reporters avoid stories that might be seen as too critical of Israel's actions. As a result, issues such as the impact of the Separation Wall on Christian communities in Bethlehem, the confiscation of Christian land for settlement expansion, and the emigration crisis facing Palestinian Christians are often overlooked or downplayed.

The absence of Palestinian Christian voices in Western media is also tied to the broader geopolitical landscape. Israel's position as a strategic ally for Western governments, particularly in the context of broader Middle Eastern politics, creates a media environment where stories that challenge Israel's policies are less likely to be covered. The Christian population in Palestine is small compared to the larger Muslim and Jewish populations, and their struggles are often seen as less politically significant in the grander scheme of the Israeli-Palestinian conflict. This marginalization is exacerbated by the fact that Palestinian Christians are often caught between two larger forces: Israeli policies of occupation and the broader Palestinian struggle for self-determination. As a minority within a minority, their specific needs and challenges are frequently overlooked.

The consequences of this political bias in media coverage are profound. Without adequate representation in the media, Palestinian Christians are rendered invisible in the global conversation about the Israeli-Palestinian conflict. This lack of visibility means that the global Christian community, particularly in the West, is largely unaware of the struggles faced by their fellow believers in the Holy Land. Western Christians, who could potentially offer support and solidarity, are often left with a one-sided understanding of the conflict that erases the experiences of Palestinian Christians. This erasure not only diminishes the global awareness of their plight but also perpetuates the conditions that allow their marginalization to continue.

Political bias in Western media also has the effect of normalizing the occupation and the policies that harm Palestinian Christians. By focusing primarily on Israel's security concerns and presenting the conflict through a narrow lens, the media legitimizes Israeli policies such as settlement expansion, land confiscation, and the restriction of movement for Palestinians, including Christians. The broader political narrative of supporting Israel's right to self-defense often overshadows the reality that these policies are contributing to the decline of the Christian population in Palestine, as more and more Palestinian Christians are forced to emigrate due to economic and social pressures.

Breaking this cycle of political bias requires a shift in how the media approaches the Israeli-Palestinian conflict. Journalists and news organizations must strive for greater balance in their coverage, ensuring that the voices of Palestinian Christians are included in the narrative. This means seeking out stories that highlight the specific challenges faced by Christian communities, such as the impact of Israeli policies on their access to holy sites, the emigration crisis, and the loss of Christian-owned land. It also means providing a platform for Palestinian Christian leaders to share their perspectives and advocate for the rights of their communities.

Ultimately, political bias in media coverage not only shapes how the world understands the Israeli-Palestinian conflict but also has real consequences for the people living under occupation. By erasing the voices of Palestinian Christians from the narrative, the media contributes to their marginalization and perpetuates the conditions that threaten their survival in the Holy Land. It is crucial for the media to move beyond political interests and provide a more accurate and inclusive portrayal of the conflict—one that acknowledges the diverse experiences of all those affected, including Palestinian Christians. Only then can a fuller understanding of the conflict emerge, one that includes the struggles and hopes of those who have long been forgotten.

Breaking the Silence: Calling for Increased Media Attention on the Struggles of Palestinian Christians

THE VOICES OF PALESTINIAN Christians have long been silenced or marginalized in the global media narrative surrounding the Israeli-Palestinian conflict. As a small but significant community with deep historical roots in the Holy Land, Palestinian Christians face unique struggles under Israeli occupation, including land confiscation, restricted access to religious sites, economic hardship, and emigration pressures. Yet, their stories are often overshadowed by the broader Jewish-Muslim dynamics that dominate coverage of the conflict. It is time to break this silence and call for increased media attention to the challenges faced by Palestinian Christians. Only through more comprehensive and inclusive reporting can the world gain a fuller understanding of the conflict and offer meaningful support to this marginalized community.

Palestinian Christians, who represent one of the oldest Christian communities in the world, have played a vital role in maintaining the Christian heritage of the Holy Land. From preserving ancient churches and monasteries to fostering religious and cultural traditions, their contributions to the region's history are invaluable. However, in recent decades, they have increasingly found themselves on the front lines of the Israeli-Palestinian conflict, suffering under the same oppressive policies of occupation that affect their Muslim neighbors. Despite their deep connection to the land, many Palestinian Christians face displacement due to the expansion of Israeli settlements and the confiscation of their land. Others find themselves isolated from their churches and holy sites due to the Separation Wall and military checkpoints, making it difficult to practice their faith freely.

The economic challenges facing Palestinian Christians are equally severe. The occupation has strangled the Palestinian economy, and

Christian communities have been hit particularly hard. In places like Bethlehem, a city with immense significance for Christians worldwide, Palestinian Christian business owners struggle to survive as tourism revenue is funneled toward Israeli-controlled enterprises. The financial pressures, coupled with political instability, have forced many Palestinian Christians to emigrate in search of better opportunities abroad, leading to a steady decline in the Christian population of the region. As the number of Christians in the Holy Land dwindles, the future of Christianity in the land where it was born becomes increasingly uncertain.

These challenges, though significant, have received minimal attention in mainstream media. Palestinian Christians are often invisible in the global conversation about the Israeli-Palestinian conflict, their struggles overshadowed by the broader political narrative that focuses on the Jewish-Muslim divide. This lack of coverage not only contributes to their marginalization but also prevents the global Christian community from understanding and addressing the unique hardships faced by their fellow believers. Without increased media attention, the stories of Palestinian Christians risk being forgotten, and the global support they need will remain out of reach.

To address this silence, the media must commit to a more comprehensive and balanced approach to reporting on the Israeli-Palestinian conflict. Journalists must actively seek out the voices of Palestinian Christians, ensuring that their experiences are included in the narrative. This means covering the impact of Israeli policies on Christian communities—such as land confiscation, settlement expansion, and restrictions on religious freedom—as well as highlighting the contributions Palestinian Christians have made to peacebuilding efforts in the region. By amplifying these stories, the media can help bring greater awareness to the plight of Palestinian Christians and encourage a more informed and compassionate response from the global community.

Increased media attention to the struggles of Palestinian Christians is not only important for raising awareness but also for fostering international solidarity. Many Christians around the world, particularly in the United States and Europe, are unaware of the challenges faced by their fellow Christians in the Holy Land. By bringing these stories to light, the media can help bridge this gap and mobilize global Christian communities to offer support. Whether through financial assistance, advocacy, or pilgrimage programs that prioritize engagement with local Palestinian Christian communities, global Christians have the potential to play a crucial role in preserving the Christian presence in the Holy Land. However, this support can only be realized if the media breaks its silence and shines a light on the struggles that have too long been ignored.

Additionally, increased media coverage can help challenge the political narratives that have contributed to the marginalization of Palestinian Christians. By highlighting the specific ways in which Israeli policies disproportionately affect Christian communities, the media can encourage a more nuanced understanding of the conflict. This can lead to more balanced public discourse and policy discussions, both within Western governments and international organizations. Rather than framing the conflict solely in terms of Jewish-Muslim tensions, the media has the power to broaden the conversation and include the voices of Palestinian Christians who have been sidelined for far too long.

Breaking the silence also means holding governments and international organizations accountable for their role in perpetuating the marginalization of Palestinian Christians. Media coverage can shed light on the policies and actions of foreign governments—particularly those in the West—that have contributed to the worsening situation for Christians in the Holy Land. By calling attention to the political and economic dynamics that undermine the rights of Palestinian Christians, the media can help create pressure for policy changes that prioritize human rights and justice for all people in the region, regardless of religion.

The struggle of Palestinian Christians is an essential part of the broader narrative of the Israeli-Palestinian conflict, and their voices must be heard. It is time for the media to move beyond the simplistic framing of the conflict as a binary struggle between Jews and Muslims and to recognize the diversity of experiences and communities affected by the occupation. By bringing the stories of Palestinian Christians to the forefront, the media can help foster a deeper understanding of the conflict and ensure that this ancient community is not forgotten.

The world needs to hear the voices of Palestinian Christians, and the media has a responsibility to amplify them. Breaking the silence is not only a matter of journalistic integrity—it is a moral imperative. It is time for the media to shine a light on the unique struggles of Palestinian Christians and to call for the global attention and action they deserve. Only then can we begin to address the injustices they face and work toward a future where all people in the Holy Land can live with dignity, freedom, and peace.

Chapter 11: Faith Under Fire: Religious Persecution and Harassment in the Holy Land

The Christian communities in Palestine and Israel face not only the hardships of occupation but also targeted harassment and religious persecution. From vandalism and arson attacks by Jewish extremists to systemic discrimination by Israeli authorities, Palestinian Christians find themselves under constant threat. These incidents are not isolated; they are part of a broader pattern of hostility that affects Christian life in the Holy Land, making it difficult for these ancient communities to practice their faith freely. Despite the significance of these challenges, their struggles are often overlooked in global discourse, leaving them vulnerable and marginalized in the land where their faith was born.

In recent years, Jewish extremists have carried out numerous attacks on Christian churches, monasteries, and properties across Israel and the West Bank. These acts of vandalism and arson are often motivated by a deep-seated hostility toward Christianity, a sentiment rooted in religious and political tensions. Many Christian churches, including historically significant sites such as the Church of the Holy Sepulchre, have been defaced with hateful graffiti or subjected to deliberate acts of destruction. In some cases, extremists have set fire to church property, causing extensive damage to sacred spaces. These attacks are not only acts of violence against physical structures but also an assault on the Christian presence in the Holy Land, a clear attempt to intimidate and weaken these communities.

The pattern of harassment extends beyond property damage. Palestinian Christians often report verbal abuse and threats from extremist groups who view their presence as a challenge to the dominance of Jewish identity in certain areas. These acts of intimidation create a climate of fear for many Christians, particularly those living in cities like Jerusalem or Bethlehem, where religious and political tensions run high. Despite the frequency of these incidents, accountability is rare. Israeli authorities are often slow to investigate these attacks, and in many cases, perpetrators go unpunished, emboldening extremist groups to continue their campaign of harassment against Christian communities.

In addition to the direct harassment by extremists, Palestinian Christians also face religious discrimination from Israeli authorities. Israel's legal framework and administrative practices frequently limit the freedom of religious expression for non-Jewish communities, including Christians. This discrimination manifests in various ways, from restrictive building permits that make it difficult to maintain or expand church properties to zoning laws that favor Jewish religious institutions over Christian ones. For example, churches in East Jerusalem and the West Bank often struggle to obtain permits to renovate or repair their buildings, while synagogues and Jewish religious schools face fewer bureaucratic hurdles. This unequal treatment undermines the ability of Christian communities to preserve their religious heritage and maintain their places of worship.

Israeli laws also limit the ability of Palestinian Christians to access justice when their rights are violated. The Israeli legal system often fails to provide adequate protection or recourse for Christians facing harassment or discrimination. Cases involving attacks on Christian property or individuals are frequently dismissed or delayed, leaving victims without a sense of closure or justice. In contrast, crimes against Jewish citizens are more rigorously pursued and prosecuted, reflecting a broader imbalance in how the legal system addresses the grievances of different religious groups. This disparity reinforces the sense of marginalization felt by Palestinian Christians, who often feel powerless in the face of institutional bias.

For many Palestinian Christians, life under occupation and constant harassment feels like a battle for survival. Living under the shadow of violence, they face the dual pressures of religious persecution and political oppression. Families are forced to endure the constant threat of attacks on their homes, businesses, and churches, all while navigating a legal and political system that offers little protection. Many Christians report living in fear, knowing that their faith makes them a target in a society where religious identity is deeply politicized.

These fears are not unfounded. Numerous stories from Palestinian Christians highlight the daily struggles of living under threat. In Jerusalem, Christian families face frequent harassment from extremist groups who challenge their right to live in certain neighborhoods, vandalize their property, or threaten their businesses. In the West Bank, Christians encounter similar hostilities, as well as the broader challenges of life under military occupation. Churches are often guarded day and night to prevent attacks, and clergy members have reported receiving death threats from extremists seeking to drive them out of their communities.

In addition to physical attacks, many Palestinian Christians face economic discrimination, which further compounds their vulnerability. Restrictions on movement, land confiscations, and discriminatory zoning laws make it difficult for Christian families to thrive economically, forcing many to consider emigration as their only option. The economic pressures, combined with the constant threat of violence, have led to a dramatic decline in the Christian population in the Holy Land, as more families choose to leave in search of safety and stability elsewhere. This exodus threatens the survival of Christianity in its birthplace, as churches and religious institutions struggle to maintain active congregations in the face of shrinking numbers.

The challenges faced by Palestinian Christians are compounded by the lack of international attention and support. Their plight is often overshadowed by the broader Israeli-Palestinian conflict, leaving them with few allies in their fight for religious freedom and protection. Global Christian communities, particularly in the West, remain largely unaware of the daily struggles faced by their fellow Christians in the Holy Land. This lack of awareness allows the persecution and discrimination against Palestinian Christians to continue unchecked, further eroding the Christian presence in the region.

Breaking this cycle of harassment and persecution will require concerted efforts from both local authorities and the international community. Israeli authorities must take a stronger stance against extremist groups that target Christian communities, ensuring that those responsible for acts of vandalism, arson, and harassment are held accountable. Legal reforms are also needed to provide greater protections for Christian property and religious rights, addressing the systemic discrimination that leaves these communities vulnerable. At the same time, international Christian organizations must raise awareness about the struggles faced by Palestinian Christians, advocating for their rights and offering support to those who are fighting to preserve their faith and heritage in the Holy Land.

The story of Palestinian Christians is one of resilience in the face of adversity, but their survival is far from guaranteed. As harassment by extremists continues and discriminatory practices by Israeli authorities remain in place, the future of Christianity in the Holy Land grows increasingly uncertain. It is crucial for the world to recognize the unique challenges faced by these communities and take action to ensure that they are not driven out of the land where their faith began. Only through increased awareness, advocacy, and protection can the Christian presence in the Holy Land be preserved for future generations.

Harassment by Jewish Extremists: Targeting Christian Churches and Properties

OVER THE YEARS, PALESTINIAN Christians have faced increasing harassment and targeted attacks by Jewish extremists in Israel and the West Bank. These acts of vandalism, arson, and harassment are part of a larger pattern of hostility aimed at diminishing the Christian presence in the Holy Land. These extremists, motivated by religious and political ideologies, often see Christians as outsiders in what they view as exclusively Jewish land. As a result, Christian churches, monasteries, and properties have become frequent targets of their aggression, leaving Palestinian Christians vulnerable and marginalized in the land of their ancestors.

One of the most notorious examples of these attacks occurred in 2015 when Jewish extremists set fire to the Church of the Multiplication of the Loaves and Fishes on the Sea of Galilee. This ancient church, which marks the site where Christians believe Jesus performed the miracle of feeding 5,000 people with just a few loaves of bread and fish, was heavily damaged by the fire. The arson attack caused significant destruction to the roof and interiors of the church, as well as to priceless religious artifacts. Hebrew graffiti was found at the scene, reading "false idols will be smashed," indicating the religious motivations behind the attack. Despite the historical and spiritual importance of the site, it took considerable time for authorities to investigate the crime, and only a few individuals were ultimately held accountable.

Similar incidents have occurred throughout the Holy Land, with Christian sites regularly defaced or damaged by extremist groups. In 2014, a wave of attacks on churches and monasteries occurred, many of which were attributed to far-right Jewish extremists. One such attack targeted the Dormition Abbey in Jerusalem, where graffiti reading "Death to Christians" was sprayed on the walls. In addition to hate speech, acts of arson have been reported at Christian institutions, often leading to the destruction of religious icons, manuscripts, and invaluable historical artifacts. These attacks serve not only as an affront to Christian property but also as a message of exclusion, aimed at driving Christians out of certain areas.

Vandalism has also been a common method of harassment. Christian cemeteries have been desecrated, with tombstones overturned and crosses defaced. In one particularly troubling incident in 2020, a Christian cemetery in Jerusalem was vandalized, with more than 30 gravestones damaged. Many of the defaced gravestones bore Christian symbols, including crosses, which were deliberately targeted. This attack left the local Christian community feeling vulnerable and disrespected, as the desecration of graves represents a profound violation of religious and cultural dignity.

Jewish extremists often target Christian religious leaders, further deepening the sense of fear and intimidation within Christian communities. Priests and monks have reported verbal abuse, threats, and even physical assaults from extremist groups. In one case, a monk from the Armenian Apostolic Church in Jerusalem was spat on by extremists as he walked through the Old City in his religious attire. Such acts of harassment are intended to humiliate and provoke fear among Christian clergy, who already face numerous challenges in maintaining their presence in a politically charged environment.

These attacks are not isolated incidents; rather, they form part of a broader campaign by Jewish extremists to assert dominance over the region and intimidate non-Jewish populations. Many of the extremist groups responsible for these attacks subscribe to an ideology that views the Holy Land as belonging solely to the Jewish people, and they seek to marginalize or drive out non-Jewish communities. Christians, alongside Muslims, are seen as obstacles to their vision of a purely Jewish state, and as such, are frequently targeted for harassment.

The response from Israeli authorities to these attacks has been inconsistent, further exacerbating the problem. In many cases, investigations into attacks on Christian churches and properties are delayed or handled with a lack of urgency. While some perpetrators have been brought to justice, many acts of vandalism and arson go unsolved, with little follow-up or accountability. This lack of enforcement emboldens extremists, who often feel they can carry out their acts of violence without consequence. The insufficient legal protection for Palestinian Christians sends a troubling message—that their safety and rights are secondary to broader political concerns.

The ongoing harassment of Palestinian Christians by Jewish extremists highlights the precarious position of the Christian community in the Holy Land. These attacks, whether through vandalism, arson, or intimidation, are not just assaults on physical properties; they are direct challenges to the very existence of Christianity in its birthplace. For many Palestinian Christians, the constant threat of harassment makes it difficult to live freely, practice their faith, and preserve their cultural and religious heritage. Without stronger legal protections and a more concerted effort by Israeli authorities to hold extremists accountable, the Christian presence in the Holy Land will continue to diminish, as more families and communities are forced to leave in search of safety and stability elsewhere.

It is critical for the international community, particularly global Christian organizations, to raise awareness of these ongoing attacks and advocate for greater protection for Palestinian Christians. The Holy Land's rich religious diversity is at risk, and the continued harassment of Christian communities threatens the future of Christianity in the region. By shining a light on these acts of extremism and calling for justice, the world can help safeguard the Christian heritage of the Holy Land and ensure that these ancient communities are not driven into extinction by violence and intolerance.

Religious Discrimination by Israeli

Authorities: Limiting Christian Freedom and Access to Justice

PALESTINIAN CHRISTIANS in Israel and the occupied territories face significant religious discrimination, not only from extremist groups but also from Israeli authorities themselves. Through a range of laws, policies, and administrative practices, the Israeli government limits the freedom of religious expression for Christian communities and creates barriers that prevent them from accessing justice when their rights are violated. This systematic discrimination undermines the ability of Palestinian Christians to live freely, practice their faith, and maintain their religious institutions in the land where Christianity was born. The effects of these policies extend far beyond daily inconveniences, as they have long-term implications for the survival of Christianity in the Holy Land.

One of the key areas where discrimination is evident is in the legal and administrative hurdles that Palestinian Christians face when it comes to maintaining, renovating, or building churches and other religious properties. Israeli zoning and building laws are notoriously restrictive, particularly for non-Jewish communities. Churches often find it nearly impossible to obtain the necessary permits to repair or expand their facilities, despite the urgent need to maintain these historic and culturally significant sites. In East Jerusalem, for example, Christian institutions have faced numerous bureaucratic obstacles in securing permits to restore churches that are centuries old, even though these sites are part of the region's rich religious heritage. In contrast, Jewish religious buildings, including synagogues and religious schools, face far fewer challenges in obtaining similar permits.

The unequal treatment extends beyond religious buildings to Christian-owned properties. In many cases, land owned by churches or Christian families has been expropriated by Israeli authorities under the guise of security concerns or development projects. This land is often handed over to Israeli settlers, further eroding the territorial presence of Palestinian Christians. One infamous example of this is the confiscation of church lands in the West Bank, where large portions of land owned by Christian institutions have been seized to make way for settlements or Israeli military infrastructure. These land grabs, often carried out with little notice or legal recourse, contribute to the gradual displacement of Christian communities from their ancestral homes.

Israeli authorities also discriminate against Palestinian Christians when it comes to the freedom of movement, particularly in relation to religious worship. The construction of the Separation Wall and the proliferation of military checkpoints in the West Bank have made it increasingly difficult for Christians to access their churches, especially during religious holidays like Christmas and Easter. Palestinian Christians living in cities like Bethlehem, which is separated from Jerusalem by the Wall, often require special permits to attend religious services at the Church of the Holy Sepulchre or other holy sites in Jerusalem. These permits are not always granted, and even when they are, Christians must pass through multiple checkpoints, where they are subject to long delays and frequent harassment. This restriction on religious freedom is a direct violation of the rights of Palestinian Christians to practice their faith freely and without hindrance.

The unequal treatment of Palestinian Christians is further exacerbated by discriminatory practices in Israel's legal system, which often fails to provide adequate protection or justice for Christian communities. When Christian properties or religious sites are vandalized, attacked, or desecrated, Israeli authorities are often slow to investigate or prosecute those responsible. Many cases of arson, graffiti, or damage to churches and monasteries go unsolved, and perpetrators are rarely brought to justice. This lack of legal accountability leaves Christian communities vulnerable to further attacks and creates a climate of fear and insecurity. In contrast, crimes against Jewish religious institutions are investigated with far greater urgency, and offenders are more likely to be prosecuted.

In addition to the lack of legal protection for Christian property, Palestinian Christians face discrimination in accessing broader legal rights. Israeli laws, such as the controversial Nation-State Law passed in 2018, explicitly prioritize the Jewish character of the state, reinforcing a system of institutionalized inequality. This law, which defines Israel as the nation-state of the Jewish people, downgrades the status of non-Jewish citizens, including Christians, effectively making them second-class citizens. Under this legal framework, the rights of Palestinian Christians to equality, justice, and religious freedom are undermined by a system that privileges Jewish identity and national interests over the rights of minority groups.

The legal and administrative barriers faced by Palestinian Christians also extend to their ability to seek redress when their rights are violated. Christian communities often find themselves marginalized in Israel's legal system, where their claims are either delayed or dismissed. For example, when churches have attempted to challenge the illegal confiscation of their land, their cases have been tied up in lengthy legal battles that can take years to resolve, if they are resolved at all. In many instances, churches have lost their cases, not because their claims lacked merit, but because the legal system is stacked against them. The lack of timely and fair access to justice for Palestinian Christians reinforces their sense of powerlessness and fuels the emigration crisis that is causing the Christian population in the Holy Land to decline.

The discrimination faced by Palestinian Christians is not limited to the legal and bureaucratic realms but also extends to broader social and political policies that favor the Jewish majority. Christian communities are often excluded from important political and social decisions that affect their lives, leaving them with little say in the policies that govern their religious and cultural practices. This exclusion, coupled with the systematic marginalization they face, contributes to the feeling that they are being driven out of their homeland, as their rights to religious freedom, property ownership, and access to justice are gradually eroded.

Despite these challenges, Palestinian Christians continue to maintain their presence in the Holy Land, but their survival is far from guaranteed. The discriminatory practices of the Israeli authorities, combined with the broader political and social pressures they face, have created an environment where it is increasingly difficult for Christians to thrive. Without stronger legal protections and a commitment to ensuring equal rights for all religious communities, the Christian presence in the Holy Land will continue to shrink, threatening the rich religious diversity that has defined the region for centuries.

To address the religious discrimination faced by Palestinian Christians, there must be a concerted effort from both local authorities and the international community to hold Israeli authorities accountable for their actions. Legal reforms are needed to ensure that Christian communities have equal access to building permits, property rights, and religious freedoms. Additionally, the international community, particularly global Christian organizations, must advocate for the rights of Palestinian Christians, raising awareness about the challenges they face and pressuring Israeli authorities to end discriminatory practices. Only through such efforts can the religious freedom and cultural heritage of Palestinian Christians be preserved, ensuring that Christianity continues to have a future in the Holy Land.

Living Under Constant Threat: The Daily Fear of Attacks on Palestinian Christians

FOR PALESTINIAN CHRISTIANS, life in the Holy Land is fraught with anxiety and uncertainty. Many live under constant threat, fearing attacks on their homes, churches, and communities by extremists who seek to intimidate and drive them away. This ongoing pressure is not only physical but also emotional, as the fear of harassment, violence, or destruction of property looms over their daily lives. These attacks, both direct and indirect, create an atmosphere of vulnerability, forcing many Palestinian Christians to question their future in the land of their ancestors. Despite their deep historical roots and commitment to maintaining their presence in the region, they face relentless challenges that make life increasingly precarious.

One of the most prominent forms of this threat comes in the form of targeted attacks on churches and religious sites. In recent years, incidents of vandalism, arson, and desecration have become alarmingly common. One Christian resident of Jerusalem, Elias, shares the ongoing fear he experiences as a caretaker of a historic church. "Every day, we worry about the safety of the church," he says. "We have seen graffiti on the walls, threats spray-painted in Hebrew, and even attempts to set fire to parts of the building. It's terrifying because we feel like we have no protection." Elias explains that while complaints are filed with authorities, little action is taken, and the attacks persist without any significant consequences for the perpetrators.

Similarly, in Bethlehem, families living close to the Separation Wall face the constant threat of their homes being attacked by extremists. Nadia, a mother of three, describes how stones are regularly thrown at her house by settlers who live nearby. "We hear the rocks hitting our windows at night. It's like they want us to feel unsafe, to drive us out of our own homes," she says. Despite the emotional toll this takes on her and her children, Nadia feels trapped. "We have nowhere else to go, and we don't want to leave the land of our ancestors. But every day, we feel less welcome here." Like many other Palestinian Christians, Nadia's family lives in fear of escalation, knowing that these smaller acts of intimidation could lead to more violent confrontations.

The fear is not limited to private homes. Churches, monasteries, and religious institutions are also frequent targets. One particularly shocking incident occurred at the Mar Elias Monastery near Haifa, where extremists desecrated the holy site, spraying offensive graffiti and causing damage to the property. The monks who reside at the monastery live in constant fear of further attacks. Father George, one of the monks, recalls waking up one morning to find hateful messages written on the monastery's walls. "We live a life of prayer and peace, but we are always afraid that our peaceful way of life will be shattered by another attack," he says. The fear of physical harm is compounded by the spiritual devastation that these attacks bring. For Father George and others like him, the desecration of sacred spaces is not just a violation of property but an assault on their faith and identity.

Beyond the physical violence, there is a pervasive sense of emotional and psychological pressure. Many Palestinian Christians report feeling increasingly isolated, both from the broader Palestinian community and from the global Christian community. They are often caught in the middle of the Israeli-Palestinian conflict, and their voices are marginalized or ignored. This isolation is exacerbated by the lack of attention given to their struggles, both in local and international media. The result is a growing sense of abandonment, as families feel that their plight is invisible to the world.

For many Christian families, this pressure ultimately leads to the difficult decision to emigrate. Hanna, a Christian shop owner in Bethlehem, explains the dilemma he faces. "My family has been here for generations, but now we are thinking of leaving. The attacks on our community, the difficulty of living under occupation, and the constant fear—it has become too much. We love our land, but we don't feel safe anymore." Hanna's story is emblematic of the broader crisis facing Palestinian Christians. As more families leave in search of safety and stability elsewhere, the Christian presence in the Holy Land continues to dwindle.

The daily threats faced by Palestinian Christians are not limited to direct violence; they also suffer from structural violence in the form of discriminatory policies and restrictions on movement. The construction of the Separation Wall and the establishment of military checkpoints have made it increasingly difficult for Christians to access their holy sites, particularly in Jerusalem. Those who live in cities like Bethlehem or Hebron must obtain special permits to visit the Church of the Holy Sepulchre or other important religious locations. For many, these permits are difficult to acquire, and even when granted, passing through the checkpoints is an arduous and humiliating experience. Father Daniel, a priest in Bethlehem, describes how his parishioners must pass through multiple checkpoints to attend services in Jerusalem. "The process is long and difficult. People are treated like criminals for wanting to worship in their own holy sites. It's degrading and makes us feel like we don't belong in the land where our faith was born."

The fear of violence and the pressure to leave have created a sense of uncertainty about the future of Christianity in the Holy Land. Despite the resilience of these communities, many Palestinian Christians feel that their existence is under threat, both from extremist groups and from broader political and social pressures. As the Christian population continues to decline, there is a growing concern that these ancient communities may one day disappear entirely from the land that has been their home for centuries.

To combat this fear and ensure the survival of Christianity in the Holy Land, there must be stronger legal protections and greater awareness of the challenges facing Palestinian Christians. Israeli authorities must take a firmer stance against the extremist groups that target Christian communities, and international Christian organizations must advocate for the protection and preservation of these communities. Without such efforts, the daily threats faced by Palestinian Christians will continue to erode their presence in the region, leaving the Holy Land devoid of its rich and diverse Christian heritage.

Chapter 12: Resilience and Hope: The Fight to Preserve Christianity in the Holy Land

In the face of immense challenges, Palestinian Christians continue to demonstrate remarkable resilience and an unshakable commitment to preserving their presence in the Holy Land. Despite the growing pressures of occupation, harassment by extremists, and the harsh realities of political and economic marginalization, Christian communities in Palestine refuse to be erased. Their fight for survival is not just a matter of defending property or cultural heritage—it is a profound spiritual struggle to maintain their faith and identity in the land where Christianity was born. Through advocacy, peaceful protests, legal battles, and the steadfast leadership of the local church, Palestinian Christians are standing their ground, drawing strength from their faith to endure and overcome adversity.

One of the most powerful ways that Palestinian Christians resist erasure is through organized efforts of advocacy and peaceful protest. These communities have long used their voices to speak out against the injustices they face, from land confiscations to restrictions on religious freedom. Peaceful protests, often centered around key religious sites or occasions such as Christmas and Easter, serve as a visible reminder to the world that Palestinian Christians are not willing to disappear quietly. In Bethlehem, for example, Christians have organized peaceful demonstrations against the expansion of Israeli settlements on church-owned lands, drawing international attention to their plight.

These acts of resistance, though peaceful, are significant acts of defiance against a system that seeks to marginalize their presence.

In addition to public demonstrations, Palestinian Christians have turned to the courts to fight for their rights. Legal battles to reclaim confiscated lands or prevent the expropriation of church property are ongoing, with many cases stretching over years, if not decades. Despite the challenges of navigating a legal system that often favors Israeli settlers, Christian communities continue to push forward with their claims, determined to defend their ancestral lands. The Greek Orthodox Church, for example, has been embroiled in long-standing legal battles over property in Jerusalem, fighting to prevent key Christian sites from falling into the hands of private developers or settlers. These legal efforts, though slow and complex, represent a critical front in the struggle to preserve Christian land and heritage in the Holy Land.

Amid these struggles, faith remains at the heart of the Palestinian Christian experience. Many Christians draw deeply on their religious beliefs to endure the daily hardships of life under occupation. Their faith provides a source of strength, hope, and perseverance, even when faced with violence, discrimination, or the constant threat of displacement. One such testimony comes from Miriam, a Palestinian Christian living in Jerusalem, who speaks of the power of her faith to sustain her. "Every day, I feel the weight of the challenges we face as a community, but my faith reminds me that we are never alone. This land has been home to Christians for centuries, and I believe we are called to stay here, to keep our faith alive, no matter the cost." For many Palestinian Christians like Miriam, faith is not only a private matter but a form of resistance in itself—a commitment to staying rooted in the Holy Land despite the odds.

The courage and resilience of Palestinian Christians is also evident in their day-to-day lives. In Bethlehem, Nablus, and other cities, Christians continue to run schools, hospitals, and charitable organizations that serve both Christian and Muslim communities alike. These institutions, many of which are affiliated with local churches, provide essential services to the Palestinian population, regardless of faith, while also preserving the Christian legacy of the region. Through their work, Palestinian Christians demonstrate a commitment to peace, coexistence, and the well-being of their society, despite the hardships they face. Their willingness to serve and to lead within their communities is a powerful testament to their enduring hope.

Church leaders play a vital role in advocating for the rights of Palestinian Christians, both locally and on the global stage. Patriarchs, bishops, priests, and pastors have been outspoken in their efforts to raise awareness about the challenges their communities face, using their positions of authority to call for justice and peace. Locally, church leaders have organized meetings with government officials, both Palestinian and Israeli, in attempts to secure protections for Christian communities and religious sites. They have also been instrumental in organizing peaceful protests and mediating legal disputes over church lands. Globally, these leaders have called on Christians around the world to stand in solidarity with their Palestinian brothers and sisters.

One notable example is the Kairos Palestine movement, initiated by Palestinian Christian leaders in 2009. This document, written as a theological and political response to the occupation, calls for global Christian solidarity and outlines a vision for peace and justice in the Holy Land. It has become a rallying cry for churches and Christian organizations worldwide to advocate for the rights of Palestinian Christians and to promote nonviolent resistance to the occupation. The Kairos Palestine document underscores the deep connection between faith and activism for Palestinian Christians, highlighting their belief that justice is central to the Christian message.

Local church leaders also work tirelessly to ensure that the Christian heritage of the Holy Land is preserved for future generations.

Many churches, monasteries, and religious institutions continue to provide spiritual and material support to Christians who remain in the region, offering a sense of stability in an otherwise uncertain environment. In addition to their spiritual duties, these leaders have become vocal advocates for peace, often calling for dialogue between Christians, Muslims, and Jews to foster mutual understanding and cooperation in a land marked by division.

The global church has begun to respond to these calls for solidarity, with increasing efforts from international Christian organizations to support the Palestinian Christian community. Pilgrimages, advocacy campaigns, and financial support have helped bring attention to the struggles of Christians in the Holy Land. Many churches abroad have adopted resolutions calling for justice in Palestine and urging their governments to take action on behalf of Palestinian Christians. These efforts, though still growing, represent an important step toward building a stronger global movement in support of the Christian presence in the Holy Land.

Despite the enormous challenges they face, Palestinian Christians remain deeply committed to their homeland and their faith. Their resilience is a testament to their belief in the importance of maintaining the Christian presence in the land where Jesus walked. Through advocacy, peaceful resistance, and unwavering faith, they continue to fight for their right to exist and to worship in the Holy Land. Their struggle is not just for survival but for the preservation of a rich religious and cultural heritage that has defined the region for centuries. It is a fight filled with hope—a hope that, despite the adversity, Christianity will endure in the land where it began.

Resisting Erasure: The Fight of Palestinian Christians to Maintain Their Presence in the Holy Land

IN THE FACE OF MOUNTING pressures and systematic marginalization, Palestinian Christians have committed themselves to resisting the erasure of their presence from the Holy Land. Despite being a minority, they have shown remarkable resilience through organized advocacy, peaceful protests, and legal battles aimed at safeguarding their land, religious sites, and cultural identity. This struggle is not just about physical survival; it is about maintaining their deep-rooted Christian heritage in the birthplace of their faith. Through persistent efforts, they continue to make their voices heard, refusing to be erased from the land where their ancestors have lived and worshipped for centuries.

One of the key ways Palestinian Christians resist erasure is through peaceful protests and public demonstrations, often centered around the preservation of their lands and religious sites. These protests are powerful statements of defiance, demonstrating their commitment to remaining in the Holy Land despite the obstacles. For instance, in Bethlehem and Jerusalem, Christian communities have organized regular protests against the expansion of Israeli settlements on church-owned lands. These settlements, which encroach on Christian-owned property, threaten to displace families and weaken the Christian presence in these historically significant areas. By protesting peacefully, Palestinian Christians draw international attention to their cause, raising awareness about the injustices they face and calling for action to prevent further land grabs.

In addition to public protests, Palestinian Christians have turned to legal avenues to resist the expropriation of their lands. Legal battles over church-owned properties, particularly in Jerusalem and the West Bank, have become a critical part of their efforts to defend their ancestral homes and religious sites. The Greek Orthodox Church, the Roman Catholic Church, and other Christian institutions have been engaged in lengthy court cases to prevent the transfer of key properties to Israeli settlers. These legal battles are often drawn-out, complicated, and costly, but they represent a vital line of defense against the erasure of Christian communities from the Holy Land.

One notable legal struggle involves the ownership of properties in Jerusalem's Old City, where Christian institutions have fought to prevent the sale of church land to private developers and settlers. In 2017, a controversial case involving the sale of properties by the Greek Orthodox Patriarchate to Israeli groups sparked outrage among the Palestinian Christian community. Local Christians saw this as a betrayal, fearing that the sale would accelerate the displacement of Christian families from the Old City. In response, they mounted legal challenges to block the sales and launched advocacy campaigns to raise awareness of the issue. These efforts highlight the broader struggle to protect Christian lands from being sold or expropriated, which is crucial to maintaining their presence in the region.

Advocacy efforts by Palestinian Christians extend beyond legal battles and protests. Church leaders and community activists have also worked tirelessly to bring international attention to their cause, calling on global Christian communities to stand in solidarity with them. The Kairos Palestine movement, launched by Palestinian Christian leaders, is one such example. The Kairos document, published in 2009, calls for justice, peace, and an end to the Israeli occupation, while urging Christians worldwide to support their Palestinian brothers and sisters. This movement emphasizes nonviolent resistance and the moral responsibility of global Christians to act against injustice. It has inspired churches around the world to take a stand for Palestinian rights and to support efforts to preserve the Christian presence in the Holy Land.

Despite these efforts, the challenges remain immense. Palestinian Christians continue to face pressure from settlement expansion, land confiscations, and discriminatory policies that threaten their ability to remain in their homeland. The construction of the Israeli Separation Wall has severed Christian communities from their agricultural lands, schools, and places of worship, further complicating their ability to live and practice their faith freely. Yet, in the face of these challenges, Palestinian Christians have shown extraordinary determination. Their efforts to resist erasure are rooted not only in their desire to maintain their homes and lands but also in their deep sense of belonging to the Holy Land, where their faith has flourished for centuries.

At the heart of this resistance is a strong sense of identity and purpose. For Palestinian Christians, remaining in the Holy Land is not simply about surviving in the present; it is about ensuring that future generations can live and worship in the land of their ancestors. The preservation of Christian institutions—churches, schools, hospitals, and monasteries—serves as a tangible connection to this heritage, providing a foundation for the continuation of their faith. These institutions play a vital role in maintaining the Christian presence in the region, offering services and support to the broader Palestinian population, regardless of religion. By supporting these institutions, Palestinian Christians contribute to the social and cultural fabric of the Holy Land, demonstrating their enduring commitment to their homeland.

Their resistance also reflects a broader commitment to coexistence and peace. Palestinian Christians have long played a role in promoting dialogue and understanding between different religious and ethnic groups in the region. Through their advocacy, they have consistently called for peaceful solutions to the conflict, emphasizing the need for justice and equality for all people living in the Holy Land. This commitment to peace is central to their efforts to resist erasure, as they believe that true peace can only be achieved when the rights and dignity of all communities are respected.

Despite the overwhelming challenges they face, Palestinian Christians remain steadfast in their resolve to resist erasure. Their peaceful protests, legal battles, and advocacy efforts are powerful expressions of their determination to maintain their presence in the Holy Land. They refuse to be silenced or displaced, and their struggle serves as a reminder of the importance of preserving the Christian heritage of the region. As they continue to fight for their rights, they embody the resilience and hope that has sustained Christian communities in the Holy Land for centuries. Through their efforts, they not only resist erasure but also reaffirm their deep connection to the land where their faith began.

Faith in the Face of Adversity: Testimonies of Palestinian Christians Standing Firm

AMID THE TRIALS OF occupation, land confiscations, and growing economic and social pressures, many Palestinian Christians continue to draw strength from their faith, refusing to leave the land they call home. For them, the Holy Land is not just a geographical space; it is the cradle of their faith, where their religious history intersects with their personal identity. Despite immense challenges, they remain, anchored by their belief in the importance of their Christian heritage and their deep connection to the land. Their testimonies of resilience highlight how faith sustains them in the face of adversity, allowing them to navigate a life filled with uncertainty, violence, and discrimination.

One such story is that of Elias, a Christian shopkeeper in Bethlehem, who has lived through decades of occupation and violence but refuses to abandon his ancestral home. "Every day is a struggle," Elias says, "but my faith gives me hope. I know that God has placed me here for a reason, and I will not leave this land, no matter what happens." For Elias, his shop is not just a business; it is a symbol of survival. Despite the hardships brought on by restrictions on movement, a declining economy, and the constant pressure from Israeli authorities, he continues to run his store, welcoming visitors and pilgrims from around the world. "It is difficult," he admits, "but every time I walk through the streets of Bethlehem, I am reminded of the deep history we have here as Christians. This is where Jesus was born. How can I leave that behind?"

Similarly, Miriam, a Christian mother of two from Jerusalem, draws strength from her faith to remain in her home city despite the many challenges her family faces. Living under occupation, Miriam has witnessed firsthand the harassment and discrimination that her community endures daily. "There are times when it feels overwhelming," she says. "The checkpoints, the permits, the fear of losing our home—it's a lot to carry. But my faith keeps me going. I believe that this land is holy, and that God has a purpose for us being here." Miriam shares how her faith is intertwined with her hope for the future, not only for her family but for the broader Christian community in Palestine. "I teach my children that we are here for a reason, that we must keep our faith alive in the land where it began. It's not just about surviving day to day; it's about holding onto our identity, our heritage."

Father George, a priest in the West Bank, offers another perspective on faith in the face of adversity. As a religious leader, he feels a deep responsibility to guide his community through the challenges they face. "Many people ask me, 'Why do you stay?' But I see it as my duty to remain here, to be a witness of faith in this land, no matter the difficulties," he explains. Father George leads a small but resilient congregation, and he speaks of how the hardships they endure only strengthen their resolve. "We are surrounded by walls and checkpoints, but our faith knows no boundaries. Every Sunday, we gather to pray for peace, not just for ourselves but for everyone in this land—Muslims, Jews, and Christians alike." His words reflect a deep commitment to both his faith and the idea of coexistence, even amid division and conflict.

Rami, a young Christian man from Nablus, describes the personal toll of the occupation but also how it has deepened his faith. "Life here can be very isolating," he says. "Sometimes it feels like the world has forgotten about us. But my faith reminds me that we are not alone, that God is with us in every step." Rami works with local youth in his community, helping to mentor young Christians who often feel disconnected or marginalized. "Many young people think about leaving," he admits. "It's hard when you see so many of your friends and family members emigrate. But I try to remind them that we have a role to play here, that our faith gives us the strength to stay and make a difference." For Rami, his faith is not just a personal comfort but a call to action—to remain in the Holy Land and to serve his community, despite the challenges.

These stories of resilience are echoed throughout the Christian community in Palestine. In the face of adversity, many Palestinian Christians hold firmly to their faith as a source of strength, hope, and identity. Whether it is in the form of small daily acts—running a shop, raising a family, or leading a congregation—Palestinian Christians are determined to preserve their heritage and continue the Christian presence in the Holy Land. Their unwavering belief that they are called to remain in the land of their ancestors fuels their perseverance, even when the world around them seems to be crumbling.

This deep-rooted faith is also evident in the way Palestinian Christians approach their future. Many speak of their hope for peace and justice, not just for themselves but for all people in the region. Their faith leads them to advocate for nonviolence, dialogue, and reconciliation, even when they are the victims of violence and oppression. For Palestinian Christians, the teachings of Christ—to love one's neighbor, to seek peace, to forgive—are not abstract principles but lived realities that guide their daily lives.

As the Christian population in the Holy Land continues to shrink due to emigration, those who remain do so with a profound sense of purpose. They see themselves as stewards of the Christian faith in its birthplace, and they believe that their continued presence is essential to preserving the region's rich religious and cultural diversity. "We are the living stones of this land," says Salwa, an elderly Christian woman who has lived her entire life in a small village near Hebron. "Our faith is what keeps us here, even when it seems like everything else is against us." Salwa's words capture the spirit of resilience that defines Palestinian Christians—a faith that endures, even in the face of adversity, because it is rooted in a profound connection to the land and the belief that their presence matters.

These testimonies are not just stories of survival; they are stories of hope. Through their faith, Palestinian Christians continue to believe in a better future, one where they can live freely and peacefully in the land where their faith began. Their resilience is a powerful reminder that, even in the darkest times, faith can provide the strength to endure, to persevere, and to hope for a brighter tomorrow.

The Role of the Church in Advocacy: Defending the Rights of Palestinian Christians Locally and Globally

IN THE MIDST OF THE ongoing challenges faced by Palestinian Christians, local church leaders have emerged as powerful advocates for their communities, both within Palestine and on the global stage. These leaders play a critical role in not only maintaining the spiritual life of their congregations but also in raising awareness about the political, social, and economic pressures faced by Palestinian Christians. By using their platforms to speak out against injustice, calling for peace and equality, and mobilizing international support, church leaders have become vital defenders of the Christian presence in the Holy Land. Their efforts are essential to ensuring that the voice of Palestinian Christians is not silenced amid the larger Israeli-Palestinian conflict.

One of the key ways local church leaders advocate for their communities is by addressing the injustices caused by the Israeli occupation. They regularly speak out against the confiscation of church lands, restrictions on religious freedom, and the broader systemic discrimination faced by Palestinian Christians. Many of these leaders have taken a public stance against the construction of Israeli settlements on Christian-owned land, particularly in areas like Bethlehem, where church properties are increasingly threatened by expansion. Patriarchs, bishops, and priests have organized meetings with Israeli officials to press for the protection of Christian lands and religious sites, and they often use their influence to mediate disputes between the Israeli government and local Christian communities.

In addition to their local efforts, church leaders in Palestine are deeply involved in global advocacy for their communities. Recognizing that the struggles of Palestinian Christians are often overshadowed by the broader conflict, these leaders have made it a priority to bring international attention to their cause. One of the most influential movements in this regard is Kairos Palestine, a Christian initiative launched in 2009 by Palestinian church leaders. The Kairos document calls for peace, justice, and an end to the Israeli occupation, urging Christians worldwide to take a stand in solidarity with their Palestinian brothers and sisters. This movement has gained significant traction, inspiring churches around the world to advocate for the rights of Palestinian Christians and to support nonviolent resistance to the occupation.

Through initiatives like Kairos Palestine, church leaders have also emphasized the moral and ethical responsibilities of global Christians. They encourage international Christian communities to pressure their governments to take a more active role in supporting peace efforts in the Holy Land and to challenge policies that perpetuate injustice. This global advocacy is vital, as it amplifies the voices of Palestinian Christians and highlights their plight to a broader audience. By engaging with churches, human rights organizations, and international forums, Palestinian Christian leaders ensure that their struggle for justice is not confined to local conversations but becomes part of a global movement for peace.

Church leaders also play a critical role in maintaining the Christian institutions that are central to the survival of the Christian community in Palestine. Schools, hospitals, and charities run by Christian organizations provide essential services to both Christians and Muslims, strengthening the social fabric of Palestinian society. These institutions are often under threat due to funding challenges and the restrictions imposed by the occupation, but church leaders work tirelessly to keep them operational. In doing so, they not only provide critical support to their communities but also preserve the Christian presence in the Holy Land by ensuring that these vital institutions remain functioning.

Locally, church leaders have been instrumental in fostering interfaith dialogue and promoting peace between Christians, Muslims, and Jews. In a region fraught with religious and political tensions, Palestinian Christian leaders have consistently advocated for nonviolent solutions to the conflict, emphasizing the need for coexistence and mutual respect. They have organized interfaith conferences, participated in peace-building initiatives, and worked to bridge divides between religious groups. Their commitment to dialogue and peace stands in stark contrast to the violence and division that often characterize the region, offering a vision of hope for a more just and peaceful future.

Church leaders also advocate for the rights of Palestinian Christians by engaging with Israeli and Palestinian authorities to address issues related to freedom of worship and access to religious sites. For instance, during religious holidays such as Easter and Christmas, Palestinian Christians often face severe restrictions when trying to visit holy sites in Jerusalem due to military checkpoints and permit requirements. Church leaders regularly petition Israeli authorities to ease these restrictions, ensuring that Christians can practice their faith without unnecessary barriers. Although these efforts often face resistance, church leaders persist in their advocacy, recognizing the importance of religious freedom for their communities.

One of the greatest challenges that church leaders face is the declining Christian population in the Holy Land, driven largely by emigration. Many Palestinian Christians, facing economic hardship, political instability, and social marginalization, have been forced to leave their homeland in search of better opportunities abroad. Church leaders are deeply concerned about this trend, as the continued emigration of Christians threatens to erase the Christian presence in the region. To address this issue, they have launched initiatives aimed at supporting Christian families who remain in Palestine, providing financial assistance, housing, and education to help alleviate some of the pressures that drive emigration. By offering these forms of support, church leaders hope to stem the tide of Christian emigration and preserve the Christian community in the Holy Land.

The global church plays a critical role in supporting the advocacy efforts of Palestinian Christian leaders. Many international churches have responded to the calls for solidarity by organizing pilgrimages, advocacy campaigns, and financial support for Christian institutions in Palestine. These efforts help to raise awareness of the challenges faced by Palestinian Christians and provide much-needed resources to sustain their communities. Moreover, the support of the global church reinforces the message that Palestinian Christians are not alone in their struggle, offering hope and encouragement to those who continue to fight for justice in the Holy Land.

Through their tireless efforts, church leaders in Palestine have become champions of justice and peace, both locally and globally. Their advocacy not only defends the rights of Palestinian Christians but also seeks to promote a broader vision of coexistence and reconciliation in a land marked by division. By raising their voices against injustice and working to preserve the Christian presence in the Holy Land, these leaders play an indispensable role in ensuring that the faith and heritage of Palestinian Christians are not erased. Their work serves as a powerful reminder of the importance of faith-based advocacy in the pursuit of peace and justice.

Conclusion: The Call for Global Christian Solidarity

The plight of Palestinian Christians has often been overshadowed by the broader Israeli-Palestinian conflict, leaving many in the global Christian community unaware of the daily struggles faced by their brothers and sisters in the Holy Land. While Palestinian Christians endure land confiscations, restrictions on religious freedom, economic marginalization, and the constant threat of violence, much of the global Christian community remains disconnected from their reality. It is time for Christians outside the Middle East to end this ignorance and take a stand in solidarity with Palestinian Christians, recognizing the urgency of their struggle for survival in the land where Christianity was born. This call to action requires not only greater awareness but also a renewed commitment to justice, advocacy, and meaningful support.

Ending the ignorance that has kept many global Christians unaware of the realities facing Palestinian Christians is a crucial first step. For too long, many Christians around the world—particularly in the West—have offered their uncritical support to the state of Israel, often without understanding the consequences of this support for the indigenous Christian population. This blind allegiance has been influenced by political and theological factors, including the rise of Christian Zionism, which views modern Israel as a fulfillment of biblical prophecy. However, this narrative overlooks the impact of Israeli policies on Palestinian Christians, who are being driven from their homes, losing access to their holy sites, and seeing their communities shrink due to emigration. It is essential for global Christians to educate themselves about the complex realities of the conflict and the unique struggles faced by Palestinian Christians, many of whom have lived in the region for centuries. By learning about these challenges, Christians can begin to engage in more informed, thoughtful discussions about the situation and reconsider their support for policies that harm their fellow believers.

Once Christians around the world are informed, the next step is to offer meaningful support to Palestinian Christians. This support can take many forms, including political advocacy, donations, and awareness campaigns. One of the most impactful ways global Christians can help is by advocating for policies that promote peace and justice in the Holy Land. This includes pressing their governments to take a more balanced approach to the Israeli-Palestinian conflict, one that recognizes the rights of all people in the region, including Palestinian Christians. Advocacy efforts can also focus on ending settlement expansion, supporting the preservation of Christian lands and institutions, and calling for greater protections for religious freedoms. By using their political influence, Christians can help shift the conversation towards a more just and equitable future for all in the Holy Land.

Donations are another practical way that global Christians can support the survival of Palestinian Christian communities. Many Christian institutions in Palestine, including schools, hospitals, and churches, struggle to survive due to the economic pressures of the occupation. Financial support from the global Christian community can help keep these institutions afloat, allowing them to continue providing essential services to the local population. Additionally, donations can be used to support legal battles to protect Christian land from confiscation or to assist families who are at risk of losing their homes. These contributions not only provide immediate relief but also help preserve the Christian presence in the region for future generations.

Awareness campaigns are equally important in ensuring that the voices of Palestinian Christians are heard. Global Christian organizations, churches, and individual believers can play a crucial role in amplifying the stories of Palestinian Christians, bringing attention to their struggles, and encouraging others to get involved. Social media, conferences, and church gatherings offer platforms where these stories can be shared, helping to raise awareness and foster solidarity across borders. The more people know about the situation, the more likely they are to engage in efforts to support Palestinian Christians and advocate for their rights.

Ultimately, the goal of this call for solidarity is to ensure a future of justice and faith for Palestinian Christians. This future is not just about survival; it is about ensuring that Palestinian Christians can live with dignity, freedom, and peace in the land of their ancestors. It is about protecting their right to practice their faith, preserving their cultural heritage, and ensuring that future generations of Christians can remain rooted in the Holy Land. Achieving this vision will require a global commitment to justice—one that transcends political divisions and focuses on the shared values of faith, compassion, and solidarity.

In this struggle, the global Christian community has a vital role to play. By standing with Palestinian Christians, Christians worldwide can help build a more just and equitable future for the Holy Land, one where all people, regardless of their religion, can live in peace. This requires a deep, ongoing commitment to advocacy, support, and education, as well as a willingness to challenge narratives that have marginalized Palestinian Christians for too long. The call for solidarity is not just a call to action; it is a call to live out the principles of faith—justice, love, and compassion—by standing with those who are suffering and ensuring that their voices are heard.

As Christians, the time has come to embrace a renewed commitment to justice for Palestinian Christians. Their struggle is our struggle, and their survival is essential to preserving the rich religious diversity and heritage of the Holy Land. By standing together in solidarity, we can help ensure that Palestinian Christians continue to thrive in the land where their faith was born, and that the Holy Land remains a place of hope, faith, and peace for all.

Ending the Ignorance: A Call for Christians to Reconsider Unquestioning Support for Israel

FOR TOO LONG, MANY Christians outside the Middle East have remained unaware of the harsh realities faced by Palestinian Christians living under Israeli occupation. As the global Christian community, it is essential to move beyond ignorance and engage with the truth about the suffering of fellow believers in the Holy Land. While political and theological narratives—particularly the influence of Christian Zionism—have led many Christians to offer their unquestioning support for the state of Israel, this support often comes at a great cost to Palestinian Christians. These communities, who are deeply rooted in the land where Christianity was born, face daily threats to their existence, including land confiscation, religious discrimination, and economic hardship. It is time for Christians worldwide to educate themselves about these challenges and reconsider their blind allegiance to Israel, understanding the broader implications of such support.

The ignorance surrounding the plight of Palestinian Christians is not entirely accidental. For years, much of the global conversation about the Israeli-Palestinian conflict has been shaped by political and religious narratives that oversimplify the situation, framing it as a struggle between Jews and Muslims. Within this narrative, Christians are often invisible, their voices and experiences sidelined or ignored. As a result, many Christians in the West have developed a narrow view of the conflict, one that paints Israel as a beacon of democracy and religious freedom, while Palestinian communities are seen through the lens of political instability or terrorism. This simplistic perspective fails to capture the full complexity of the situation and, more importantly, neglects the suffering of Palestinian Christians who are caught in the crossfire.

A major factor contributing to this ignorance is the rise of Christian Zionism, a theological movement that sees the modern state of Israel as the fulfillment of biblical prophecy. For many Christian Zionists, supporting Israel is not just a political stance; it is a religious obligation. This belief has been widely promoted in churches and Christian organizations, particularly in the United States, where millions of Christians are taught that standing with Israel is equivalent to fulfilling God's will. However, this theological framework often overlooks the real-world consequences of Israeli policies on Palestinian Christians. By prioritizing Israel's political interests, Christian Zionists unwittingly support policies that oppress their fellow Christians in the region.

It is crucial for Christians around the world to confront this ignorance by educating themselves about the true experiences of Palestinian Christians. These communities are not outsiders; they are native to the Holy Land and have lived there for centuries, maintaining a continuous Christian presence since the early days of the church. Today, they find themselves facing immense challenges: their lands are being confiscated to make way for Israeli settlements, their access to religious sites is restricted by military checkpoints, and their economic opportunities are severely limited by the occupation. Many Palestinian Christians are forced to leave their homeland, leading to a steady decline in the Christian population in the Holy Land.

One of the most urgent issues facing Palestinian Christians is the confiscation of their land. In cities like Bethlehem and Jerusalem, large portions of church-owned lands have been taken by the Israeli government, often under the guise of security concerns or development projects. These lands are then used for settlement expansion, further displacing Christian families who have lived there for generations. The construction of the Separation Wall has also severed many Christian communities from their agricultural lands, cutting them off from vital resources and economic opportunities. This land loss is not just a matter of property; it threatens the very survival of the Christian presence in the Holy Land, as more families are driven out by economic hardship.

Religious freedom is another area where Palestinian Christians face significant discrimination. Despite Israel's claims to protect religious liberty, Palestinian Christians often encounter severe restrictions when trying to access their holy sites, particularly in Jerusalem. During important religious holidays such as Christmas and Easter, Palestinian Christians living in the West Bank must obtain special permits to enter the city and worship at sites like the Church of the Holy Sepulchre. These permits are not always granted, and even when they are, Christians must pass through multiple military checkpoints, where they are subjected to long delays, searches, and harassment. This systematic restriction on religious freedom makes it difficult for Palestinian Christians to practice their faith and maintain their connection to the holy sites that are central to their identity.

The economic challenges facing Palestinian Christians are equally dire. Living under occupation has crippled the Palestinian economy, and Christian communities, many of whom depend on tourism and agriculture, have been hit particularly hard. The restrictions on movement, combined with the loss of land and resources, have left many Christian families struggling to survive. As a result, an increasing number of Palestinian Christians are choosing to emigrate, seeking better opportunities abroad. This emigration poses a serious threat to the future of Christianity in the Holy Land, as the Christian population continues to shrink with each passing year.

For global Christians, these realities should be a wake-up call. The blind support for Israel that has been promoted in many churches ignores the suffering of Palestinian Christians and contributes to their marginalization. It is time for Christians to reevaluate their theological and political stances, recognizing that standing with Israel does not necessarily mean supporting justice for all people in the region. True solidarity with the Holy Land must include standing with Palestinian Christians, advocating for their rights, and ensuring that their voices are heard.

This process of education and reevaluation starts with listening to the stories of Palestinian Christians themselves. Global Christians must seek out these voices, whether through church leaders, advocacy organizations, or direct engagement with Christian communities in Palestine. By learning about their struggles, Christians can develop a more nuanced and compassionate understanding of the conflict—one that takes into account the full range of experiences in the region. This knowledge can then be used to inform political advocacy, pushing for policies that protect the rights of Palestinian Christians and promote peace and justice for all people in the Holy Land.

Ending the ignorance also requires Christians to challenge the narratives that have contributed to their unquestioning support for Israel. This means critically examining the theological assumptions of Christian Zionism and recognizing that support for Israel's political actions should not come at the expense of justice for Palestinian Christians. It also means holding Israeli policies accountable, advocating for an end to settlement expansion, the protection of religious freedoms, and the preservation of Christian lands and institutions.

Ultimately, ending the ignorance is about creating a more just and equitable future for Palestinian Christians. It is about ensuring that they are not erased from the land where their faith was born and that they can live with dignity, freedom, and security. By educating themselves and standing in solidarity with Palestinian Christians, global Christians can play a vital role in preserving the Christian presence in the Holy Land and advocating for a future of peace and justice for all.

Supporting the Struggle: How Global Christians Can Offer Meaningful Help

AS PALESTINIAN CHRISTIANS face increasing pressure from occupation, economic hardship, and threats to their religious freedom, global Christian communities are called to action. The struggle for justice, dignity, and survival in the Holy Land is not only a local issue but one that demands global solidarity. Christians around the world can offer meaningful support to their Palestinian brothers and sisters through political advocacy, financial donations, and awareness campaigns. By standing together, the global Christian community can help ensure that Christianity remains rooted in the land where it was born and that Palestinian Christians can continue to live and worship freely.

One of the most impactful ways global Christians can support Palestinian Christians is through political advocacy. The policies that affect Palestinian Christians are shaped not only by the Israeli government but also by the international community. Many Western governments, particularly in the United States and Europe, have strong political and economic ties to Israel, which often leads to a lack of accountability for the actions that harm Palestinian communities. Christians worldwide can use their influence to advocate for policies that promote peace and justice in the Holy Land, urging their governments to take a more balanced approach to the Israeli-Palestinian conflict. This includes pressing for an end to Israeli settlement expansion, calling for the protection of Christian lands and institutions, and demanding that religious freedoms for all people in the region be upheld.

Political advocacy can take many forms, from writing letters to elected officials, participating in public demonstrations, and engaging in dialogues with policymakers. Christian organizations and churches can also play a vital role by lobbying for policy changes that reflect a commitment to justice and equality for Palestinian Christians. By speaking out against unjust policies and advocating for a fair and lasting peace, global Christians can help create the political pressure needed to bring about real change in the Holy Land.

Another critical way global Christians can support the struggle of Palestinian Christians is through financial donations. Many Christian institutions in Palestine, such as schools, hospitals, churches, and charitable organizations, are under immense financial strain due to the occupation and the declining Christian population. These institutions provide essential services not only to Christians but also to the broader Palestinian community, fostering coexistence and peace. However, the ongoing economic challenges make it difficult for these organizations to continue their work. Donations from Christians around the world can provide much-needed resources to keep these institutions running, ensuring that they can continue to serve their communities and preserve the Christian presence in the region.

In addition to supporting institutions, financial contributions can also be directed toward legal aid for Palestinian Christians who are fighting to protect their lands from confiscation. Legal battles over church-owned property and Christian-owned land are long, costly, and complicated, but they are crucial for preserving the Christian heritage of the Holy Land. Donations to organizations that provide legal assistance can help level the playing field, giving Palestinian Christians the resources they need to defend their rights in court.

Financial support is also vital for families who are struggling to remain in Palestine amid growing economic pressures. Many Christian families face the difficult decision of whether to emigrate in search of better opportunities, but with financial support from the global Christian community, they may be able to stay and maintain their ties to the Holy Land. Donations can help provide housing assistance, educational opportunities, and small business support, offering a lifeline to families who wish to remain in their homeland.

Raising awareness about the challenges faced by Palestinian Christians is another powerful way the global Christian community can offer support. Awareness campaigns are essential for educating Christians around the world about the realities of life for their brothers and sisters in the Holy Land. For too long, the struggles of Palestinian Christians have been overlooked or overshadowed by the larger Israeli-Palestinian conflict. Through social media, church networks, and Christian organizations, global Christians can help bring attention to these challenges, ensuring that the voices of Palestinian Christians are heard.

Churches can organize awareness events, including educational seminars, conferences, and guest speakers from Palestinian Christian communities. By inviting Palestinian Christian leaders to speak directly to their congregations, global Christians can gain a more personal and nuanced understanding of the situation. These events also provide opportunities to build solidarity and foster relationships between Christians across borders. Additionally, social media platforms offer a way for Christians to share information, stories, and advocacy campaigns with a broader audience, helping to spread the message of solidarity far and wide.

Christians can also participate in pilgrimages to the Holy Land, but with a focus on supporting local Palestinian Christian communities. Many pilgrimages are organized in ways that benefit Israeli businesses and settlements, bypassing Palestinian Christian-owned hotels, restaurants, and shops. By choosing pilgrimage tours that prioritize engagement with local Palestinian Christians, global Christians can ensure that their visits provide economic support to the communities that need it most. These pilgrimages can also serve as opportunities for Christians to witness the realities of the occupation firsthand, gaining a deeper understanding of the challenges faced by their Palestinian brothers and sisters.

Lastly, Christians can support Palestinian Christians by participating in ecumenical and interfaith initiatives that promote peace and reconciliation in the Holy Land. Many Christian organizations, such as Kairos Palestine, have called for nonviolent resistance to the occupation and for Christians worldwide to advocate for a just peace. By joining these initiatives, Christians can work together to build bridges of understanding and solidarity, both within the global Christian community and with other religious groups in the region. These efforts are crucial for creating a broader movement for peace that includes all people of faith in the Holy Land.

In conclusion, global Christians have a vital role to play in supporting the struggle of Palestinian Christians. Through political advocacy, financial donations, and awareness campaigns, they can help ensure that Palestinian Christians have the resources and support they need to survive and thrive in the Holy Land. This is not just about offering charity; it is about standing in solidarity with fellow Christians who are fighting for their right to exist in the land where their faith began. By taking action, Christians worldwide can help preserve the Christian heritage of the Holy Land and work toward a future of justice, peace, and coexistence for all people in the region.

A Future of Justice and Faith: Renewing the Global Commitment to Palestinian Christians

AS THE CHRISTIAN PRESENCE in the Holy Land continues to face existential threats, it is imperative that the global Christian community recommits itself to justice and solidarity with Palestinian

Christians. Their struggle for survival in the birthplace of Christianity is a challenge not only to their local community but to the global Christian faith itself. Without the active engagement of Christians worldwide, the rich religious and cultural heritage of Palestinian Christians risks being lost to the forces of occupation, economic hardship, and displacement. Now, more than ever, there is a need for global unity in supporting their right to live freely and practice their faith in the land where Christianity was born.

A future of justice for Palestinian Christians begins with recognizing the scale of the challenges they face. Their situation is not merely a political or social issue but a deeply spiritual one. They are the stewards of a faith tradition that has been rooted in the Holy Land for centuries, and their ability to remain there is essential to preserving the Christian presence in the region. The forces that threaten them—from the expansion of Israeli settlements to restrictions on religious freedoms and the loss of land—are steadily eroding the Christian population in Palestine, leaving many to wonder if Christianity can survive in the land of its birth. This is not only a local crisis; it is a global one that affects the entire Christian community.

The call for justice is grounded in the fundamental principles of Christian faith—love, compassion, equality, and the pursuit of peace. Justice for Palestinian Christians means ensuring that they are not marginalized or displaced but are given the same rights and protections as all people living in the Holy Land. This includes the right to practice their religion freely, to have access to their holy sites, to own and protect their land, and to live without the fear of violence or oppression. Justice is not a passive hope for change; it requires active participation and advocacy from Christians around the world.

Global unity in this struggle is essential. For too long, the plight of Palestinian Christians has been overshadowed by the broader Israeli-Palestinian conflict or overlooked altogether. Many Christians outside the Middle East remain unaware of the daily struggles faced by their fellow believers in the Holy Land, often due to the lack of media coverage and political complexity of the region. However, the global Christian community cannot afford to be passive or silent any longer. Unity in purpose and action is necessary to ensure that Palestinian Christians do not disappear from the land where Christianity began.

This global unity must be expressed through tangible actions, not just words of solidarity. Christians around the world must engage in political advocacy, pushing their governments to support peace initiatives that protect the rights of all people in the region, including Palestinian Christians. This means calling for an end to settlement expansion, ensuring that Palestinian Christians have access to their holy sites, and advocating for policies that promote coexistence and mutual respect between different religious communities. By advocating for a just and equitable solution to the Israeli-Palestinian conflict, global Christians can help create a future where all faiths can thrive in the Holy Land.

Moreover, the global Christian community must also support Palestinian Christians on a personal and institutional level. This includes financial support for Christian schools, hospitals, and churches that are struggling to remain open due to the pressures of occupation and economic instability. These institutions are vital not only to the Christian community but also to the broader Palestinian population, as they provide education, healthcare, and spiritual guidance to people of all faiths. By sustaining these institutions, global Christians can help ensure that Palestinian Christians can continue to serve their communities and maintain their presence in the Holy Land.

In addition to advocacy and financial support, global Christians must foster awareness about the situation of Palestinian Christians. This can be done through education campaigns, church programs, and pilgrimages that focus on engaging with local Christian communities in Palestine. Raising awareness is crucial to building a global movement that understands the challenges facing Palestinian Christians and is committed to supporting their survival. By sharing their stories and amplifying their voices, Christians around the world can help bring greater attention to the injustices they face and build momentum for meaningful change.

A future of justice and faith for Palestinian Christians is not just about preserving a religious minority—it is about protecting the very heart of Christianity. The Holy Land is a place of profound significance for Christians worldwide, and the continued presence of Palestinian Christians is a living testament to the enduring legacy of the faith. Their survival in the face of adversity is a powerful reminder of the resilience of faith, and it is a challenge to all Christians to stand in solidarity with them. By renewing the global commitment to justice, Christians can help ensure that the Holy Land remains a place of faith, hope, and peace for generations to come.

This renewed commitment requires courage, persistence, and unity. It calls on Christians to look beyond political divisions and national boundaries and to focus on the shared values of justice, compassion, and faith. It is a call to action for churches, Christian organizations, and individual believers to come together and advocate for the rights of Palestinian Christians, recognizing that their struggle is part of a broader fight for peace and justice in the world. Only through collective effort and a unified voice can the global Christian community ensure that Palestinian Christians are not forgotten and that their future is one of dignity, freedom, and faith.

In this moment, Christians worldwide are faced with a choice: to remain passive in the face of injustice or to take up the call for solidarity and justice for their fellow believers. The future of Palestinian Christians depends on the global Christian community's willingness to stand with them, to fight for their rights, and to ensure that their presence in the Holy Land endures. It is a future worth fighting for, one that honors the principles of faith and justice that lie at the core of Christianity. Let this be a moment of renewed commitment to building a future where Palestinian Christians can live freely, practice their faith without fear, and continue to serve as stewards of Christianity in the land where it all began.

Appendix

1. **Key Historical Events Impacting Palestinian Christians**

○ A timeline of significant historical events that have affected Palestinian Christians, such as the establishment of the State of Israel in 1948, the Six-Day War in 1967, and the ongoing settlement expansions.

○ Explanation of how these events have led to the displacement and marginalization of Palestinian Christians, along with the loss of their lands and restricted access to holy sites.

2. **Important Christian Sites in Palestine and Israel**

○ A detailed list of key Christian holy sites in the Holy Land, including the Church of the Nativity in Bethlehem, the Church of the Holy Sepulchre in Jerusalem, and the Mount of Olives.

○ Descriptions of the religious significance of these sites and the challenges Palestinian Christians face in accessing and maintaining them under occupation.

3. **Israeli Laws Affecting Palestinian Christians**

○ A breakdown of key Israeli laws and policies that disproportionately impact Palestinian Christians, such as the Absentee Property Law, discriminatory zoning laws, and restrictions on freedom of movement.

○ Analysis of how these laws facilitate the confiscation of Christian lands and hinder religious freedoms for Palestinian Christians.

4. Christian Denominations in the Holy Land

○ An overview of the different Christian denominations present in Palestine and Israel, including Orthodox, Catholic, and Protestant communities.

○ Discussion of their unique traditions and contributions to the Christian heritage of the Holy Land, as well as the challenges each denomination faces in maintaining their presence.

5. Glossary of Terms

○ A glossary of key terms related to the Israeli-Palestinian conflict and Palestinian Christians, such as "Nakba," "Intifada," "Christian Zionism," and "Separation Wall."

○ Definitions and explanations of these terms to provide readers with a clearer understanding of the context surrounding the struggles of Palestinian Christians.

6. Global Christian Organizations Supporting Palestinian Christians

○ A list of international Christian organizations, NGOs, and churches that are actively involved in supporting Palestinian Christians through advocacy, donations, and awareness campaigns.

○ Contact information and resources for readers who wish to get involved or contribute to these efforts.

7. Further Reading and Resources

○ A curated list of books, articles, documentaries, and online resources that provide deeper insight into the situation of Palestinian Christians, the Israeli-Palestinian conflict, and Christian advocacy for justice in the Holy Land.

○ Recommendations for both historical and contemporary works that offer perspectives on the challenges facing Palestinian Christians and the broader political and religious dynamics of the region.

8. Interviews and Testimonies

○ Transcripts of interviews and personal testimonies from Palestinian Christian leaders, clergy, and laypeople who have shared their experiences of living under occupation and maintaining their faith in the Holy Land.

○ These testimonies offer a personal, human perspective on the themes discussed in the book, highlighting the resilience and faith of Palestinian Christians.

9. Sample Letters for Advocacy

○ Templates for letters that readers can send to their local representatives, church leaders, or international organizations advocating for the rights of Palestinian Christians.

○ Guidance on how to effectively communicate the importance of supporting Palestinian Christians through political, financial, and spiritual means.

10. Statistics on Palestinian Christians

○ Data on the declining population of Palestinian Christians in the Holy Land, including statistics on emigration, land confiscation, and restricted access to religious sites.

○ Analysis of the impact of these trends on the future of Christianity in the region and the importance of global support for Palestinian Christians' survival.

www.ingramcontent.com/pod-product-compliance
Lightning Source LLC
Chambersburg PA
CBHW051522150726

47997CB00001B/355